HUMAN ELEMENTS TRAINING FOR EMERGENCY SERVICES, PUBLIC SAFETY AND DISASTER PERSONNEL:

AN INSTRUCTIONAL GUIDE TO TEACHING DEBRIEFING, CRISIS INTERVENTION AND STRESS MANAGEMENT PROGRAMS

Jeffrey T. Mitchell, Ph.D.
George S. Everly, Jr., Ph.D.

Critical Incident Stress Debriefing: (CISD) An Operations Manual for the Prevention of Traumatic Stress Among Emergency Services and Disaster Workers

Jeffrey T. Mitchell and George S. Everly, Jr.

Emergency Response to Crisis - A crisis intervention guidebook for emergency service personnel

Jeffrey T. Mitchell and H. L. P. Resnik

Occupational Health Promotion - Health Behavior in the Workplace

George S. Everly, Jr. and Robert H. L. Feldman

RESCUE! - Community Oriented Preventive Education Handbook - Helping children cope with stress

Ofra Ayalon

Human Elements Training For Emergency Services, Public Safety and Disaster Personnel:

An Instructional Guide to Teaching Debriefing, Crisis Intervention and Stress Management Programs

Jeffrey T. Mitchell, Ph.D.
George S. Everly, Jr., Ph.D., F.A.P.M.

CHEVRON
Publishing Corporation

CHEVRON Publishing Corporation

5018 Dorsey Hall Drive, Suite 104

Ellicott City, MD 21042

Editorial / production supervision
and interior design: *Robert E. Bramhall*

Cover Photo Courtesy of the Maryland State Police

CHEVRON

Publishing Corporation

1994 by Chevron Publishing Corporation
Ellicott City, MD 21042

ISBN: 1-883581-01-X

Printed in the United States of America

Dedications

To my Dad,
Who taught me to teach...
Who taught me to work...
Who taught me to swim, to camp, and to live healthy...
Who, in the end, gave me a better than passing grade on my early
life by summarizing my childhood with the words, "You were
a good child; Such a nice child!".
To my Dad,
The finest instructor I ever knew.

(JTM)

To Andrea Newman Everly;
with love and the hope that the world that you will know will
have a greater understanding of the "human elements".

(GSE)

Acknowledgments

Writing acknowledgments always appears to be among the most monumental features of book writing. One never knows exactly where to begin or how far to go. Authors are faced with dread over the very real possibility of leaving someone out of the list of those to be thanked. The task is even further complicated when there is more than one author, as is the case with this book. But, something must be said because no book reaches completion without the assistance of other people beside the authors.

With that cautious introduction in mind, we now set about the task of attempting to thank the many who have given so much to us as we labored over this project. It seems most fitting that we first thank our families and others who love us. They tolerated our absences, distractions, mood swings and some level of neglect as the book writing continued over these many months.

Thanks go to our many students over the years who continuously taught us what we had forgotten about teaching. Particular appreciation goes to the adult learners who attended our conferences and workshops and who were so generous in their suggestions and comments.

Special thanks goes to Bruce Walz, Ph.D. of the Emergency Health Services Department of the University of Maryland. He read several of the chapters, made important suggestions and offered considerable guidance. His remarks were adhered to and the end product is far better than it would have been without him.

Maggie and Greg Valcourt also played important roles in the development of this text. They frequently challenged us and made suggestions and comments which kept us thinking, changing, correcting and reformulating. Many times they did not even know that they were influencing us so heavily.

And police officers, fire fighters, nurses, paramedics, life guards, search and rescue teams, corrections officials, ski patrollers, physicians, wild land fire fighters, natural resources personnel and members of the armed forces should be thanked for their encouragement that they offered us on this project. Their continued expression of the need for us to provide this manual made it ultimately happen.

Thank you to all of you named and unnamed. We appreciate every thing you have said or done to make this book a reality.

Jeffrey T. Mitchell
and
George S. Everly, Jr.

TABLE OF CONTENTS

CHAPTER 1

Key Concepts in Critical Incident Stress Management

INTRODUCTION

Traumatic stress reactions have been recognized since the times of antiquity. The earliest records of traumatic stress reactions are associated with endeavors such as warfare. The twentieth century is the century not only of the formal recognition of post traumatic stress reactions within the official nosologies (APA, 1980), but post traumatic stress was also recognized in this century as a possible occurrence far from the fields of war (APA, 1987).

The specific scope of the problem of post traumatic stress reactions is very difficult to assess, yet some recent efforts have been made to quantify the extent of the problem. Cummings and Vanden Bos (1981), for example, estimate that in excess of sixty percent (60%) of all visits to health care professionals are for stress related complaints. Schor (1991) indicates that adults report experiences of "high stress" nearly every day. There is a well entrenched popular belief that the emergency services professions are capable of generating high levels of psychological trauma. In support of this belief, Corneil (1993) discovered that over 16% of fire fighters in a large metropolitan fire department in Canada had experienced post-traumatic stress reactions as a result of their emergency work. Finally, Freudenheim (1987) has estimated that job stress costs the American economy in excess of $150 billion annually.

Significant progress has been made in developing both an understanding of the nature of traumatic stress and a series of prevention and intervention techniques designed to mitigate the impact of post trauma stress. The following sections will review some of what is known about psychotrauma and the most effective methods to deal with the problem.

PSYCHOTRAUMATOLOGY

The impact that distress in general, and post traumatic stress, specifically, has upon society is certainly worthy of debate. Yet most will probably agree that the stress impact is deleterious and significantly widespread. Indeed, excessive stress may be capable of ending a career, or even a life (Everly, 1989).

In 1992 the American Red Cross created a disaster mental health service to provide mental health services to primary and secondary victims of disaster. In the same year, the American Psychological Association created its disaster response network to assist victims of natural and man-made disasters with the consequences of these traumatic events. Within the latter part of this last decade we have witnessed the emergence of a virtually new field of emergency response.

Donovan (1991) suggested that the term "traumatology" be used to unite the various endeavors within the field of traumatic stress studies. Figley (1993) agrees and uses the term traumatology to define "the investigation and application of knowledge about the immediate and long-term psychosocial consequences of highly stressful events and the factors which affect those consequences" (p. xvii).

As Donovan (1991) himself notes, however, the term "traumatology" denotes the branch of medicine that deals with wounds and serious injuries. For this reason Everly (1992; Mitchell and Everly, 1993) has suggested that the term "psychotraumatology" be used to denote this new field of psychological trauma. More specifically the term psychotraumatology can be a more precise description for the study of the factors antecedent to, concomitant with and subsequent to, psychological traumatization (Everly, 1993).

CRITICAL INCIDENT STRESS

If we use the term psychotraumatology as an umbrella term

which implies the general field of psychological trauma, we can now turn to specific branches of the term. A sub term in the field of psychotraumatology is "traumatic stress". This term is often used to denote the stress response which follows traumatization. It appears to have its origin in combat related stress reactions.

The term, "critical incident stress" (CIS) is a term which has emerged from paramilitary and public safety agencies to describe the essence of the traumatic stress response which occurs beyond the "battlefield" as it might be encountered by law enforcement, fire suppression, emergency medical, industrial and even civilian personnel. In recent years the two terms, traumatic stress and critical incident stress have been used synonymously.

In order to respond to the challenge that critical incident stress places upon the numerous emergency services and public safety professions, the field of critical incident stress management (CISM) was born. The critical incident stress management field contains many specialized critical incident stress prevention and intervention techniques. They include, but should not be limited to:

* Pre incident stress education

* A well organized CISM team

* Chaplain programs

* Support programs for significant others

* Family life services

* Administrator / supervisor education

* Peer counseling

* Community outreach and education programs

* On scene support services

* Individual consultations

* Defusings

* Critical Incident Stress Debriefings (CISD)

* Disaster services

* Follow up services

* Informal discussions

* Professional referral services

* Mutual assistance programs for other organizations

* Other services as required

The centerpiece of most CISM programs and probably the most well publicized of the CISM services is the intervention technique known as the critical incident stress debriefing (CISD).

DEFINING CISD

Initially developed by the senior author (Mitchell, 1983; Mitchell, 1988 a, b; Mitchell and Bray, 1990; Mitchell and Everly, 1993) as a means of preventing or mitigating traumatic stress (critical incident stress), CISD has become what many consider the most widely used technique in the world for the prevention of work-related traumatic stress (CIS). Since its formulation and first applications in 1983, CISD has grown into a virtual crisis intervention subspecialty of its own. It has expanded beyond its original applications to police officers, fire fighters, paramedics, emergency medical technicians and nurses to many other professions. CISD is utilized in commercial and industrial settings, schools, community groups and in every branch of the military in at least seven other nations. There are no less than three hundred and fifty organized CISD teams throughout the world. The educational and service needs of these CISD teams are largely supported by a nonprofit educational and training foundation (The International Critical Incident Stress Foundation, Inc.) as well as numerous state and local training networks.

The Critical Incident Stress Debriefing is defined as a group intervention technique applied subsequent to a traumatic event (critical incident). It is designed to achieve two main goals:

- *Mitigate the impact of a traumatic event*
- *Accelerate the normal recovery process of healthy people who have been exposed to very unusual events*

Several studies have already been performed to examine the CISD process and to determine its effectiveness. The results of these early studies are encouraging and have further intensified interest in the usefulness of the CISD process and its applications to various traumatized groups (Dyregrov and Mitchell, 1992; Robinson and Mitchell, 1993; Rogers, 1993).

Although considerable research is still necessary to develop a full understanding of the limitations and benefits of CISD, it is believed, by many of those who have extensively utilized CISD, that the process may be instrumental in preventing or limiting post traumatic stress reactions and possibly even Post Traumatic Stress Disorder (Hytten and Hasle, 1989; Alexander, 1990; Leeman-Conley, 1990).

The CISD is soundly based in crisis intervention and educational principles which have been developed by Gerald Caplan, Erich Lindemann and others since the early forties (Parad, 1965; McGee, 1974; Kliman, 1978). The process was not designed as a form of psychotherapy, nor is it considered a substitute for psychotherapy. Mitchell and Everly (1993) have written a detailed account of the nature and basic operating guidelines of the CISD. Such a discussion is beyond the scope of this current work. The purpose of this book is to offer some general recommendations concerning training and research guidelines relevant to CISD.

CORE CONCEPTS IN CISD

A critical incident stress debriefing (CISD) is a group meeting in which a traumatic event is discussed in a non threatening and structured manner. The CISD is provided by a specially trained team which includes at least one mental health professional and several peer advisors or peer support personnel (if it is applied to emergency services personnel or to military units). "Peers" are medical, emergency service, or military personnel who have also received training in CISD/CISM. In some situations, such as when a debriefing is applied to commercial, industrial or school settings, peers may not be required. In addition, other adjustments may need to be made when applications of the CISD process are utilized with groups other that military or emergency services units. For example, it will be necessary to assure that the CISD intervention utilizes age appropriate language and techniques if the CISD is going to be used in a school system.

A CISD is structured in that it follows a specific seven phase outline. Crisis intervention techniques are integrated with critical incident stress education and information throughout the entire process. The CISD system has been designed to gently move a group from their more cognitively defended positions to one in which they are able to discuss the emotional aspects of a traumatic situation. The group is then restored to the cognitive defenses which are so necessary in the work place. The structure of the CISD helps the participants to organize their thinking and compare their experiences with others without feeling threatened by either the CISD team or the process itself. The seven phases of the debriefing are:

- **INTRODUCTION**
- **FACT**
- **THOUGHT**
- **REACTION**
- **SYMPTOMS**
- **TEACHING**
- **RE-ENTRY**

Each phase has a specific purpose and each has been carefully ordered to facilitate maximal discussion of the traumatic incident.

The debriefing process has been organized around the most natural manner in which operations personnel experience and evaluate the traumatic events of their work. It is natural for people who are used to emergency services operations to discuss their traumatic stress in a specific manner which starts with a discussion of what happened before moving onto how they feel about the event. It is also natural for operations oriented people to desire to return to a cognitive level of function which assists them in the performance of difficult tasks. Such individuals often believe from personal experience that the presence of strong emotions may interfere with the performance of their duties. The following chart depicts the specific phases of the debriefing and the mental process which is occurring during each phase:

Phase	Process	
Introduction	Cognitive	
Fact	Cognitive	
Thought	*Cognitive* ——▶	*Affective*
Reaction	Affective	
Symptoms	*Affective* ——▶	*Cognitive*
Teaching	Cognitive	
Re-entry	Cognitive	

The CISD was developed for use after extremely stressful events. It was never meant to be used with routine incidents. Too frequent a use of the debriefing may deteriorate its power and cause it to be less effective. Examples of traumatic events which are eligible for a debriefing include, but are not limited to:

- Line of duty deaths
- Serious line of duty injuries
- Suicides of emergency personnel
- Disasters
- Law enforcement shootings
- Accidental injuries to others caused by one's actions
- Significant events involving children
- Knowing the victim of a traumatic event
- Prolonged incidents which end in a loss
- Events with excessive media interest
- Life threatening experiences
- Severe abuse
- Homicides
- Terrorism
- High publicity crimes of violence
- Any significant event which overwhelms usual coping

CISD interventions appear to work best when they are provided reasonably close to the time of occurrence of the traumatic incident. The usual time frame is between twenty four and seventy two hours following the incident. Shorter or longer time frames after the traumatic incident have been utilized when circumstances warranted an earlier or later approach. What is far more important than the time frame of the support service is the fact that the group is ready to accept a debriefing when it is applied. If people are not ready for assistance, the chances for failure of the intervention will intensify.

ESSENTIAL ELEMENTS IN TRAUMA RECOVERY

Rapid intervention is only one important element in effective debriefing services. There are generally eight key components to successful crisis intervention by means of a CISD. They are:

- Rapid intervention
- Stabilization of the situation
- Mobilization of personal and organizational resources
- Getting traumatized people to talk about the trauma event
- "Normalization" of the experience
- Restoration of the social network
- The provision of practical stress management information
- Return to normal operational functions as soon as people are able

Rapid Intervention

Rapid intervention has been discussed above. There are, however, some additional points which should be made. Since operations personnel may tend to be cognitively biased, they frequently have not been able to process any of the emotional aspects of a traumatic event for the first twenty four hours. Debriefings are normally withheld for roughly the first twenty four hours. Instead, a quick defusing is provided and individual consultations are arranged until the entire group is ready to benefit from the debriefing. It is far better to provide the debriefing within the first week after the incident than to wait two or three weeks, with the obvious exceptions of mass disasters and prolonged incidents that may last days or weeks themselves.

Stabilization

Stabilization of the crisis situation is vital in recovery from psychotrauma. Chaos and confusion must be brought under control before the person or group's ability to cope deteriorates even further.

Stabilization is achieved by reducing stimulation, mobilizing outside resources, reorganizing the group or by taking control of decision making until the individual or group is ready to resume these tasks. Any effort to bring order to a chaotic situation will go far to promote a more rapid recovery of the traumatized personnel.

Mobilization

Resource mobilization is the next key element in psychological recovery from a traumatic experience. The CISD helps the person and the group to see more clearly their own personal strengths and the strengths of the group. Once they see that they have personal resources available, they often set these resources to work to recover from the traumatic situation. Frequently the organization is triggered into effective action when the immediate effects of the debriefing become apparent. In some case the participants in the debriefing give the CISD team authorization to talk to the administration of the organization and stir them to make decisions which will assist their personnel.

Verbalizing the Trauma

It has long been recognized that talking about traumatic events lowers symptoms of psychological arousal and moves people toward recovery. Over a hundred years ago, Pierre Janet pointed out that a person's ability to recover from traumatic situations was based upon the person's ability to express their emotions and to integrate the experience with their overall life by verbally exploring the trauma (van der Hart, Brown and van der Kolk, 1989). Lang (1971) showed that stress arousal lowers when people discuss their traumatic experiences. Pennebaker and Susman (1988) found that not only arousal declined when people discussed traumatic events, but the immune system's functioning was enhanced.

Normalization

"Normalization" of the traumatic event is achieved when the group is able to openly discuss the traumatic event and each sees that he or she is not alone in their reactions and that others in the group are also experiencing the same physical, cognitive, emotional, and behavioral reactions. The CISD team confirms this impression in the teaching phase of the debriefing. Team members also use one on one contacts after debriefings to confirm the fact that people are experiencing normal reactions to abnormal events.

Restoration of Social Networks

When stressful traumatic events occur, people tend to withdraw from others and box themselves into a protective position (Hann, 1985). They often become so self focused that they are unable to see that the situation has had negative effects upon those around them who were also exposed to the trauma. Recovery depends heavily on the reorganization of the disrupted social network. The social group has a significant role to play in healing, but it cannot play out this role if it is seriously disrupted (Yalom, 1985). CISD helps to restore the functions of the social network.

Stress Management

In the few evaluation studies of the debriefing process which have been performed to date, one component usually receives praise - the fact that practical instructions are given to help the traumatized personnel recover (Rogers, 1993; Dyregrov and Mitchell, 1993; Robinson and Mitchell, 1993). The debriefing gives people a sense of direction and specific guidelines which help them to make coordinated efforts to reach recovery.

Return to Normal Functions

The CISD process urges personnel to resume their ordinary tasks as soon as they are able. The CISD never urges disability claims, premature retirements or the use of sick time. Instead, CISD encourages people to function as they did before or even better than they had before the critical incident. Once people assume normal duties, they feel more in control of their situation and are usually able to reduce the symptoms of distress which are affecting them. The sense that they can carry on and that the traumatic event has not incapacitated them does much to enhance their overall recovery.

BASIC CISD PRINCIPLES

The CISD process can best be understood if the following principles are kept in mind:

- CISD was designed for use after extremely traumatic events
- CISD is a group process
- CISD is not psychotherapy
- CISD is not a substitute for psychotherapy
- CISD will not repair long standing psychiatric disorders
- CISD will not repair serious social problems
- CISD is a team approach
- CISD should only be provided by those who are CISD trained
- CISD is rooted in crisis intervention theory
- CISD mitigates the impact of the critical incident
- CISD accelerates the normal recovery process after trauma
- CISD is peer driven with mental health guidance
- CISD is a group discussion of a traumatic incident
- CISD is only one step in a process of recovery from trauma
- CISD has both emotional support and educational elements

- CISD does not require anyone to speak
- CISD is primarily prevention oriented
- CISD can be used by industries, schools, communities, etc.
- CISD must be followed up by other support services
- CISD is not an operations critique
- CISD is a short term process
- CISD is a limited approach
- CISD may enhance a person's willingness to accept help
- CISD provides the opportunity for informal assessment or screening

CONCLUSION

This chapter has discussed the concept of psychotraumatology and its subset, critical incident stress. It also described the intervention technique called the Critical Incident Stress Debriefing (CISD). Core concepts and the basic application principles of the CISD were presented along with a list of the seven phases of the CISD process. The chapter discussed the essential elements which are important in the recovery from traumatic stress. Reasons why these elements are so important were also presented.

The next chapter discusses important information on the need for course standardization and the essential qualities of instructors. The chapter also discusses the typical profile of students taking crisis and stress classes. Later chapters will cover teaching outlines for various course configurations and fundamentals of research in the CISM field.

CHAPTER   2

CISM Instructors and Students

INTRODUCTION

As more instructors enter the Critical Incident Stress Management (CISM) training and education arena, variations in training procedures, instructor styles and course content are inevitable. Some of the variations are constructive and appropriate. But, excessive variation in CISM training and education may lead to confusion, disorganization, and significant discrepancies in the quality of the programs and the services provided. Standardization in training and practice assures a greater degree of reliability in the application of CISM principles and procedures and lessens the chance that individuals will be harmed by excessive variations from a generally accepted educational format or set of application techniques.

The following training standards and the course outlines in subsequent chapters are presented in an attempt to provide greater cohesiveness in the CISD training offered to mental health, clergy and peer debriefers. Ideally, the benefits of standardization are many, in the opinion of the authors:

- **Standardized training enhances coordination and cooperation.** It enables debriefing team members from various locations to work together when they have been called upon to provide support to communities outside of their own. This is especially important in a large scale disaster in which many CISD teams would be working together.

- **Standardized training improves communications.** Standardized training insures that the debriefers use the same terminology and avoid the confusion which arises when people talk about the same processes using different terminology.

- **Standardized training increases reliability.** Standardization in training insures that the same procedures will be applied for an incident which occurs in one jurisdiction as would be applied if the incident had happened in another jurisdiction.

- **Standardization aids research efforts.** Standardization is important from the point of view of evaluation of services. It is impossible to reliably measure the effectiveness of the debriefing process if everyone is providing that service in a different manner.

Effective CISM services are seldom accidental. They are planned and organized. Most importantly, effective services only come about when the people who provide those services have been adequately trained and educated according to established and accepted standards. This chapter should help those involved in training debriefers to do the job most effectively. It, and the chapters which follow, present information on the topics which should be included in the Basic CISD (entry-level) course. The material which follows also contains many useful suggestions for those who teach virtually any aspect of Critical Incident Stress or crisis information.

INSTRUCTOR QUALIFICATIONS

The choice of an instructor to present material on Critical Incident Stress (CIS) or Critical Incident Stress Debriefing (CISD) should be an extremely careful one. The demands of teaching critical incident stress information are significant. It is not an easy topic to present to emergency services personnel who have little familiarity with the topic and even less care for it because they may perceive it to be too theoretical. Poor delivery of the information or, worse yet, faulty information can have adverse results.

The usual audience for a CIS education program is mixed. Typically, fire, rescue, law enforcement, nursing, physician, clergy and mental health personnel can be found simultaneously in the audience. This is especially so when a basic CISD course is being provided. It is very difficult to teach these mixed groups and assure that each person leaves the session with a feeling that they have each learned something. Instructor skill and knowledge will need to carefully blended to assure a satisfactory outcome of an educational program.

It is recommended that a highly qualified peer emergency services instructor with both substantial CIS and classroom experience be coupled with a skilled mental health clinician who is also well versed in the art of education to deliver the CIS or CISD material. It is also recommended that those who instruct have been trained in formal teacher education or instructor education programs in addition to extensive training and experience in the field of peer support services or clinical mental health services.

There are many aspects of the CISD course which are difficult to teach to emergency personnel unless the instructor has such experience. Peer instructor involvement in the course presentation is essential. Likewise, there are many complex or theoretical clinical mental health issues which come to the surface during the training and these often, can only be answered by qualified mental health professionals. It is a rare individual who will be able to adequately address the issues from two very different perspectives. Since it is unrealistic to expect most instructors to have both backgrounds, the teaching team of mental health professionals and peer support personnel is a highly recommended approach.

It is **not** recommended that any person teach CIS or CISD material unless they have had considerable experience in the field. It is difficult to establish an exact number of debriefings which gives a person a sufficient amount of exposure to the debriefing model to be able to teach the material. People may advance beyond the basic CISM concepts by supplementing actual CISD exposures with on scene support services, defusings, individual consultations, significant other support services and other CISM activities. A good rule of thumb, however, is that people should not teach these concepts without the experience of at least *fifteen* to *twenty five debriefings* . The exposure to that many debriefings would go far in preparing an instructor to teach CISM information to others. The concepts in themselves are not so difficult to understand. What is more difficult is the application of those concepts to real life crises. Teaching others to have flexibility in the application of the CISM concepts is also a difficult task. Even the very best instructor who functions without the practical knowledge which is developed by real life experiences in the field of CIS and CISD will have difficulty when he or she attempts to teach such material to others.

The following is a summary of minimal credentials which a CIS or CISD instructor should possess before teaching CISM concepts.

Peer Emergency Services Instructor:

1) Formal instruction in education or training methods

2) Basic and Advanced CISD courses as well as Peer Counselor/ Support training

3) Between fifteen and twenty five debriefings

4) Demonstrated knowledge of the subject matter

5) Approval to instruct by the sponsoring agencies

6) At least five years as an emergency services provider

7) Active membership on a CISD team

8) At least three letters of recommendation from organizations which have utilized the instructor

9) At least 1 year of teaching experience with emergency personnel

10) Commitment to stick with the basic CISD course concepts / outline. Adaptations should only be made when it is necessary to meet special local needs that may be unique in certain areas or in certain cultures

Mental Health Instructor:

1) A minimum of a Master's degree from a mental health training program offered by an accredited college or university

2) Basic and Advanced CISD courses as well as Post Traumatic Stress Disorder coursework or training

3) Between fifteen and twenty five debriefings

4) Formal course work in education or an equivalent experience in teaching or training

5) At least three years of clinical experience in the mental health field

6) Approval to instruct by sponsoring agencies

7) Active membership on a CISD team

8) At least three letters of recommendation from organizations which have utilized the instructor

9) At least 10 "ride along" field observation sessions split between fire services, emergency medical services, police agencies, hospital emergency departments, dispatch centers and other emergency service organizations.

10) Commitment to stick with the basic CISD course concepts / outline. Adaptations should only be made when it is necessary to meet special local needs which may be unique to certain areas and cultures.

At times, special experiences may provide an enhanced background for potential instructors and some of those experiences may partially substitute for a few of the requirements cited above. Exceptions should be made very carefully on a case by case basis. Deviations from the norm without sufficient reason will only dilute the quality of the programs which are offered to emergency personnel and may set the foundation for psychological harm to those people. An overall concern for any CIS or CISD educational program should be the best in **quality, accuracy and delivery**.

QUALITIES OF EXCELLENT INSTRUCTORS

There are many ways to describe an excellent instructor. Instructor textbooks provide a variety of lists and most people, who have spent a considerable amount of time on the student side of the desk, can tell you their own list of instructor qualites (and deficits). This section will remind instructors of things they have probably heard before about instructing. But, these reminders of simple, well known concepts often influence instructors to provide a high quality presentation in the classroom.

Lists of the most commonly identified qualities of excellent instructors usually include:

- Desire to work with people

- An understanding of people

- A desire to teach

- Knowledge and competence in the subject

- Teaching "know how"

- Enthusiasm and motivation to teach

- Ingenuity and creativity in presentation

- Empathy with the students

- Respect for the dignity of the students

- Concern for the students

- Fairness in the treatment of the students

- Strong leadership qualities

- Effective supervision abilities

- A well developed sense of humor

- The ability to be flexible

- Confidence without being arrogant

- Communication skills

- Patience

- Self control

- Self discipline

- Honesty

- Humility

- The ability to say, "I do not know"

- Willingness to ask for help

- The ability to look people in the eye

- Organization

- Ability to demonstrate the tasks required of students

- Willingness to learn more

(Weimer, Parrett and Kerns, 1988; Bachtler, 1989; IFSTA, 1981; Adkins, 1991)

Any instructor who has a wide range of these characteristics either naturally or by training and practice will have a high potential to be a great teacher.

DISTRACTIONS AND MANNERISMS TO AVOID

There are of course some teaching pitfalls to avoid. Each of these can detract from effective presentations:

- Rambling presentations

- Poor preparation

- Unfamiliarity with subject matter

- Lack of real world experience in subject matter

- Unusual (or bizarre) dress.

- Excessive pacing
- Barriers between the student and instructor
- Jargon, profanity and cliches.
- Excessively elaborate visuals
- Round-a-bout answers to direct questions
- Nervousness and fidgeting
- "Playing" with keys or coins or other objects
- Sarcasm
- Complaining
- Excessive story telling
- Speaking too fast / too slow
- Bluffing
- Bullying
- Comedy routines where serious subjects are taught
- "OK", "Ah", "YA Know", etc.

(Weimer, Parrett and Kerns, 1988; Bachtler, 1989; IFSTA, 1981; Adkins, 1991)

THE CISM / CISD STUDENTS

All education is made up of an interaction between the instructor and the learner. The sections above describe the qualifications and characteristics of good instructors. This section will round out the educational process by describing the typical learners who will interact with the instructors in CISM or CISD training programs.

A wide range of students attend Critical Incident Stress Management education programs. Occasionally CISM team members are asked to present information to the general public who have survived disasters or who have been victims of various traumatic events. These groups are usually mixed groups with a wide range of needs and issues. They may listen silently to the lecture material or they may become upset as their memories of the painful experience come to the surface as a result of the reminders which are brought forward by the lecture material. In such a case, it is best to have additional CISM team members available who can take the affected individuals outside and calm them down by listening individually to their pain. Instructors would be wise to confine their presentations to general topics which are applicable to traumatized victims. Appropriate topics might include the basic elements of disaster psychology, child or elder care, restoring routines, calling for help and the common signs and symptoms of distress which might arise as a result of the tragedy.

When the instructor is presenting CISM information to a homogeneous group such as a group made up of all police officers, or all paramedics, or entirely of nurses or only fire fighters, the task of teaching is made much easier. It is very important, however, that the instructor be familiar with the job and the needs of the student group. It will probably be necessary to alter one's audiovisuals to assure that the particular group is being addressed properly. Examples which directly related to the specific group are also important.

Instructors who are dealing with a mixed group of emergency personnel such as nurses, paramedics, fire fighters, and law enforcement personnel who are being trained together, face a somewhat greater challenge. We believe the core personalities of the various emergency personnel tend to be quite similar. The jobs, however, are very different. The students might understand the concepts which are presented in CISM training. But, they may have difficulties in making specific CISM applications to their particular profession. Sometimes there is a degree of competition or even mistrust which exists between varied professional groups. Rarely will long standing problems between professions be solved in an educational setting. Instructors should not set up such unrealistic goals for their time with the students. Awareness of pre-existing conflicts will help the instructor to avoid areas of unusual sensitivity between groups. Examples which are applicable to each group will help to alleviate this barrier to learning.

Probably the greatest challenge to CISM instructors is the teaching of a basic entry level CISD course. There is a great deal of information to present in a limited period of time and the audience is not an easy one. In most cases the peer support personnel and the mental health professionals are trained all together. There are clear advantages to the mixed training format. One of the most important is that from the outset, a CISM / CISD team is trained together. This forces very different professional groups to work together to share experiences and learn the techniques of debriefing and other CISM intervention techniques.

Along with the advantages come some considerable difficulties. Mental health understanding of the helping process may be quite different from the understanding held by peer support personnel. The sensitivities to various stimuli may be quite different for mental health professionals and emergency personnel. The difference in the levels of education between the two groups is usually significant. In addition, there may be other problems associated with mixed groups in CISD training programs. For example, some in the training may have experienced a very powerful traumatic incident. The material presented in the debriefing training tends to bring the old memories to the surface. The CISD instructor is often called upon to serve in a listener, helper or peer counselor role during breaks in the training process.

There are some helpful guidelines which will assist the CISM instructor when the students are from diverse populations. They are:

- Know the backgrounds of students

- Know the jobs of the students

- Teach so that every one comes away with something

- Treat all students as individuals

- Do not favor one group's position over another's

- Respect the dignity of each student

- Avoid generalizing the behaviors of one member of a group to the entire group

- Make sure that groups do not feel under attack
- Treat every member of the class fairly
- Set up an environment of trust and respect
- Teach concepts in such a manner that different groups can see how the same concepts can apply equally to their own circumstances
- Listen equally to opposing sides of issues
- Once the positions have been stated invite the differing parties to meet together later to discuss the issues and then move on with the class
- Use gender neutral language
- Emphasize the common themes which come up in the material
- Expect differing viewpoints and accept those
- Bridge opposing points of view whenever possible

(Billingsley, 1993)

CHALLENGES TO BE FACED IN CISM EDUCATION

It takes more than just a knowledge of the subject matter to teach well (Simpson, 1991). A primary challenge is a proper blend of the best elements of teaching skills and solid educational foundation. This book has not been written as an instructor training manual. Instead it was written as a tool for experienced instructors who are now in the position of training their personnel in CISM or CISD. New stress concepts, which are unfamiliar to many in the emergency services, will demand some adjustments in the approaches utilized by instructors.

Another challenge associated with teaching stress principles is the capacity to adapt to the emergency personnel themselves. A disregard for the emergency personnel establishes the potential for a failed educational opportunity. Guest speakers, who are, at times, unfamiliar with emergency personnel will often attest to the difficulties of teaching emergency personnel. They have reported feeling out of place and somewhat threatened by operations personnel who might be a "little rough around the edges" or "confrontative".

Our experience leads us to believe that prototypic emergency workers tend to be action oriented people who are attracted to exciting, interesting work which varies from day to day and which is also associated with elements of intrigue, challenge and danger. They tend to be driven to perfection in their job performance and are able to pay a great deal of attention to details if they perceive that the details are essential to their jobs. They are finely tuned to obtaining rewards from internal sources such as personal satisfaction. Doing their "very best" is a significant motivator. The typical emergency worker likes to be in control of him or her self and prefers also to maintain some degree of control over the environment (that includes the learning environment). They appreciate instructors who seek feedback from them so that they feel that they have some say in the learning experience (IFSTA, 1981; GP Courseware, 1983; Bachtler, 1989; Mitchell and Everly, 1993; FEMA, 1991).

Emergency personnel (especially the experienced ones) have often developed a set of protective mechanisms which assist them in tolerating the demands of the job. Among these protective mechanisms is a well developed sense of humor. A guest lecturer or new instructor who does not take that sense of humor (which can be somewhat "earthy" on occasion) into consideration is in for a distressing or, at least, a surprising experience.

Another commonly used defense mechanism which is utilized especially when and instructor is trying to teach "human elements" material is denial. Emergency personnel may resist exposing or discussing their emotions that make them feel vulnerable. This is especially so if their feelings are brought out before their peers. They therefore generally state that they have no "feelings" related to a specific situation. Only the unwise educator would press them for a disclosure of their feelings when they are clearly resisting further openness and discussion about things which are personal to them. On the other hand, when they choose to open up and voluntarily get involved in discussions about their feelings, the learning experience can be very powerful for everyone in the room (including the instructor).

Gaining the emergency workers interest and maintaining it are no easy tasks. A dry monologue on stress will kill the topic and make it aversive to an average person. The same type of presentation to a group of emergency services personnel angers them and may produce very caustic feedback, a rejection of the information and possibly the instructor. Additional training in the human elements is not very likely if the first opportunities to teach the material are badly managed. The information presented in a crisis or stress management course must be practical, interesting and easy to understand. The instructor must be lively and enthusiastic about the topic.

Another challenge facing stress or crisis instructors is the amount of stress material which is available. There are literally thousands of books and articles on general stress, but much less on critical incident stress and debriefings. It is difficult to provide comprehensive information without getting carried away in an ocean of unnecessary details. The stress instructor must work hard to organize the most essential information to be presented in a limited period of time.

Another point to consider is the difficulties associated with teaching the veterans who have a great deal of experience. The topics of stress management, crisis intervention, critical incident stress, debriefing and on scene support services may be reasonably new topics to veteran personnel. As previously mentioned, some may have developed strong denial tactics and resist the idea that they may be suffering the after effects of stress in their own lives. They may tend, therefore, to discount the value of stress education and insist that it is an unnecessary waste of time and energy. Some continue to believe that stress management is only for "wimps who should not be in the service anyway".

Tact, patience, subject knowledge, persistence and a positive delivery style can make all the difference in the world between a failed presentation and a successful one. One point to make to veteran personnel is that because they have already developed good coping or survival skills for their job, they may not feel that they need stress management information. They might be able, however, to use the information which is being presented to either improve their own survival tactics or to help a fellow worker in organizing their own survival skills.

It is best not to argue with people who think that they cannot benefit from stress education. Instead, let them know that besides using the material for self-help, they can use the information to benefit their fellow workers.

One final challenge to the stress instructor is the difficulties which are at times involved in convincing administration that stress education is good for the organization and the individuals within it. Since stress management is a somewhat intangible entity, it is difficult to measure its effectiveness. The instructor needs to spend some time reading through a wide range of materials to gather enough information to effectively counter the arguments of administrators, who simply do not have the facts about stress management.

CONCLUSION

Obviously, there are many challenges in store for the CISM / CISD instructor. There are many talents blended into the one person who teaches. Good instructors need to be knowledgeable, insightful, creative, perceptive, sensitive to their students , and driven toward excellence. They need to know their students. This is especially so when working with emergency personnel. Most of all, good instructors must be very good listeners. In listening, instructors learn and then they teach more accurately.

The challenges to good instruction are indeed many, but, they are not insurmountable. The best advantages which lessen the problems facing instructors include knowledge, confidence, and an extensive level of real world experience. Another key advantage for the CISM instructor is a clear knowledge of the personalities, the jobs and needs of the students. That knowledge can help to assure success in CISM

/ CISD education. In general, though, it will usually be most effective to have the basic entry-level CISM / CISD course team taught by a peer emergency service worker and a mental health professional.

CHAPTER   3

Teaching Human Elements Concepts: An Overview

INTRODUCTION TO "HUMAN ELEMENTS"

The emphasis in emergency services training programs is almost universally on the technical aspects of law enforcement, fire fighting, emergency medical services, nursing, search and rescue, disaster services and other forms of emergency work. This is certainly understandable for this is the essence of those fields.

What is frequently overlooked, however, is specialized training in the "*human elements*" which are also an intricate and vital component of emergency work. *Human elements* training includes such items as crisis intervention training so that personnel might be better prepared to provide assistance to those they are serving during an emergency (Mitchell and Resnik, 1981,1986; Hafen and Frandsen, 1985). *Human elements* training also includes programs in general stress management, critical incident stress management (CISM) and critical incident stress debriefing (CISD) (FEMA, 1991). *Human elements* training should also provide information on assertiveness training, conflict resolution, human communications skills, verbal negotiation skills and disaster mental health services (Harrison, 1977; Fay, 1988; Reese and Horn, 1988; Myers, 1990).

This chapter will focus on the core issues and aspects of teaching *human elements* concepts especially when the students are from the emergency services professions or are related to CISD teams. It has been primarily developed to assist emergency services instructors with their obligation to provide such information to their students in both new recruit classes and in service education programs.

DUTY TO TRAIN IN HUMAN ELEMENTS

The word "obligation" in the last sentence of the previous paragraph was no accident. The emergency organizations, regardless of their organizational orientation (police, fire, emergency medical or other emergency services agency) have a moral, ethical and professional obligation to provide training to their personnel which helps them to survive their careers and maintain their health. This includes human elements training.

Stress management heads the list of human elements training which is necessary for operations personnel. Few careers in life can cause as much distress to the personnel who work in them as the emergency services professions. Too often healthy people enter those professions only to retire (sometimes prematurely) with broken spirits, damaged bodies, disturbed home lives, changed personalities and lost dreams. The toll, in human terms, is catastrophic, but the real catastrophe is that much of that distress might be mitigated or prevented if the proper stress management and crisis intervention courses were taught.

Emergency personnel deserve and need training in stress control. Instructors have an obligation to provide it as effectively as possible.

THE STRESS EDUCATION STRATEGY

The word "strategy" implies the overall plan or the "big picture". When an emergency oriented instructor is considering a training strategy for his or her organization, the word comprehensive should be foremost in mind. A comprehensive training strategy for an organization, of course, has a great deal of emphasis on training for the everyday operational aspects of the work. But, it is also very important that a broad spectrum of human elements training be built into the recruit and in service training strategy. Many courses allow small portions of human elements training to be incorporated into the regular curriculum. Other human elements training, such as CISD will require specific blocks of time dedicated to specific courses.

Organizations need to make appropriate amounts of time available to accomplish the necessary human elements training. It should not compete with other essential training programs but should be seen as a parallel tract with equal importance.

The first aim of the strategy should be to train the entire department. Upper level commanders and immediate supervisors should be given stress management and critical incident stress training. Likewise, every member of the department should be given stress training. Without adequate stress information, personnel and their commanders will be poorly equipped to take effective steps to mitigate stress by identifying those with the chronic and acute stress conditions early enough to obtain the right kind of help. Without knowledge of stress symptoms supervisors may also miss the cues which imply that their personnel may need a referral for special assistance.

The inclusion of mental health professionals either as part of the teaching team or at least as a referral resource is highly encouraged. When emergency services workers meet mental health professionals who work with their departments, the usual misunderstandings and misconceptions about mental health professionals can be avoided or reduced.

The following is a partial list of the types of human elements training programs which can be developed for emergency organizations:

- General stress management

- Cumulative stress reactions

- Crisis intervention

- Human communications

- Family stresses

- Critical Incident Stress

- Conflict resolution

- Significant other stress

- Critical Incident Stress Management

- Critical Incident Stress Debriefing

- Command officers course on CIS

- Utilizing support resources

Again, some of these programs can be incorporated into the ongoing training normally provided by emergency organizations. This can be accomplished by small alterations in the length of the existing course or by the substitution of human elements training for less important aspects of the currently existing courses. Others will need to be developed into stand alone courses. In some cases, the resources of the department cannot afford a full program. In those situations, some personnel might need to be sent to specialized training courses in order to develop the skills they need for application within their own departments (Mitchell and Bray, 1990; FEMA, 1991)

ENVIRONMENT

It is a well known fact that people can learn under a wide range of circumstances. But, that does not mean that we should haphazardly allow instruction to take place in just any place. Some circumstances are far better for learning than others. The environment can either enhance or diminish the ability to learn. Sometimes people will have to work harder to learn because the environment is incorrect. The learning environment should not be left to chance. It should be chosen because it provides the right atmosphere to make teaching an easier process for the instructor and learning an easier process for the students. Environments which enhance learning should assure that they are:

- Free of distractions

- Uninterrupted spaces

- Scheduled to maintain priority placements for classes over other activities

- Arranged for optimum benefit of students

- Utilizing comfortable chairs and writing tables

- Equipped with adjustable lighting, heat or air conditioning

- Safe environments

(Fay, 1988; Bachtler, 1989; IFSTA, 1981; GP Courseware, 1983)

ADULT LEARNERS

Adults learn differently than children. They formulate less dependent relationships with their instructors than do children. They are used to being self directed and they should be expected to take greater responsibility for their learning. Adults are also more experienced than children in the general aspects of life. They are more prone to relate their experiences to the information they are learning. They are also more likely to participate actively in discussions. The instructor can frequently tap into the experiences of the adult learners and the entire class can benefit.

Adults also have reached a greater level of maturity and they have a greater readiness for learning than do children. They also have a greater fear of failure in developing new skills. Adults also want to be able to apply their learning immediately. They see education as a means to enhance their overall competency. What they learn needs to be directly associated to their roles and responsibilities in life. The following list identifies some of the characteristics of adult learners:

- autonomous and self directing

- task oriented

- fear of failure, may discourage easily

- anxious and more cautious of new experiences

- lacks confidence

- somewhat resistant to change
- self esteem based on past experience and achievements
- expects the best instruction
- lacks recent study experience

    (GP Courseware, 1983)

The best techniques to enhance adult learning include:

- Encouraging open discussion when possible
- Point out specific goals and objectives
- Establish the relevance of the course content
- Discourage excessive competition
- Foster personal sense of achievement
- Provide frequent reinforcement
- Provide opportunity for early success
- Provide for over learning through ample opportunities for practice
- Minimize distractions
- Emphasis their "need to know" the concepts they learn
- Respect their age and experience
- Be well prepared for class sessions
- Be patient as learners establish their learning patterns

    (GP Courseware, 1983)

ELEMENTS OF LEARNING

Learning is defined as "a change in behavior that occurs as a result of acquiring new information and putting it to use through practice." (IFSTA. 1981; GP Courseware, 1983). What is learned is processed though the mind in an ordered fashion. Information is first received by the senses. Then important elements of the information are selected by the mind and unimportant elements of the material are ignored. The information selected is entered into the short term memory where it is temporarily stored until it is organized and matched with previous information and eventually stored in long term memory. Then information can be retrieved for various purposes including the transfer of information to new experiences and to performance of skills.. A final step in the learning process is feedback which then confirms what has been learned (GP Courseware, 1983).

It is important to point out some important summary information which has been developed by educational research over the years:

HOW WE LEARN

- 1% through tasting
- 1.5% through touching
- 3.5% through smelling
- 11% through hearing
- 83% through seeing

(IFSTA, 1981, p. 28)

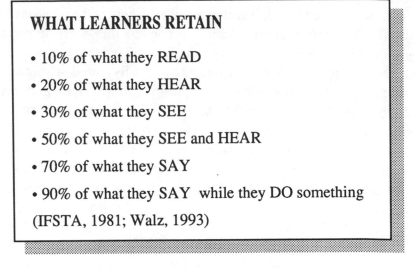

WHAT LEARNERS RETAIN

- 10% of what they READ
- 20% of what they HEAR
- 30% of what they SEE
- 50% of what they SEE and HEAR
- 70% of what they SAY
- 90% of what they SAY while they DO something

(IFSTA, 1981; Walz, 1993)

DOMAINS OF LEARNING

A famous educator in the 1950's, Benjamin Bloom, developed a classification system for the various types of learning. The system is known as "Blooms taxonomy". Bloom divided all learning in three basic areas or domains:

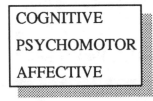

COGNITIVE
PSYCHOMOTOR
AFFECTIVE

There is another way to say that. We can think of *Knowledge, Skills and Attitude*. In fact, it is possible to put an equal sign between the two groups of domains. For example:

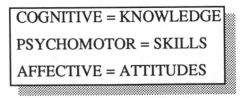

COGNITIVE = KNOWLEDGE
PSYCHOMOTOR = SKILLS
AFFECTIVE = ATTITUDES

Bloom pointed out that each of the general domains of learning could be subdivided into smaller categories. He ordered these sub categories in ascending order. Learners achieve the lowest level first before moving onto the next level. The cognitive domain has the following categories:

Knowledge - ability to recall facts

Comprehension - ability to explain or categorize information

Application - ability to apply knowledge

Analysis - ability to break a concept down into basic elements

Synthesis - ability to combine elements to form concepts

Evaluation - ability to judge the value of information and to problem solve.

As noted above, these levels of learning are arranged from simplest to most complex. Learning is a step by step process and students cannot be expected to skip stages in the process or the start with the most complex of the processes first. In teaching stress and crisis concepts, like most other types of learning, it is very important to lay a proper foundation which starts with the facts and then progresses up through the levels of learning (Harrison, 1977; GP Courseware, 1983; Bachtler, 1989; Jacobs and Chase, 1992).

The psychomotor domain or skills domain is most associated with applications of learning. This domain is typically employed when people are learning eye - hand coordination skills. The psycho-motor domain is subdivided in the following manner (from least difficult to most difficult):

Observation - learner watches an experienced person perform

Imitation - learner tries to model instructor's behaviors

Manipulation - learner attempts task based on instructions not observations

Precision - learner practices and develops skill

Perfection - learner perfects skill, functions more independently

Judgment - learner functions independently. Can judge how new skills can be applied to new situations.

The affective domain of learning is most associated with attitudes and values. Teaching in this domain is by far the most difficult of all types of teaching. Like the cognitive and psychomotor domains of learning, the affective domain has its own set of steps by which people learn in that domain. Those steps are (from easiest to most difficult):

Receiving values - learner sees or hears about the values to be learned

Respond to values - learner respond to the value presented

Accepts the values - learner accepts the values

Organization - learner organizes the values

Characterization - learner's behavior is controlled by the values

Judgment - learner is now able to apply these values to new situations

(Harrison, 1977; IFSTA, 1981; GP Courseware, 1983; Fay, 1988; Bachtler, 1989; Walz, 1990; Jacobs and Chase, 1992).

NOTE: There is much more which could be said about the cognitive , psychomotor and affective domains of learning. But, it is not the intent of this book to be a complete guide to teaching. Instead, it is designed to remind instructors of core concepts they previously learned in their instructor training courses. This book also provides a viewpoint which is clearly oriented toward teaching stress and crisis intervention topics to emergency personnel and disaster workers. For additional information on educating emergency personnel the following resource material is suggested:

Bachtler, J.R. (1989). Fire Instructors Training Guide, 2nd Edition. New York, NY: Fire Engineering, A Pennwall Publication.

Fay, J. (1988) Approaches to Criminal Justice Training. Athens GA: Carl Vinson Institute of Government, University of Georgia.

GP Courseware (1983). Fundamentals of Classroom Instruction, Vol. 1. Columbia, MD: General Physics Company

Harrison, L.H. (1977). How to teach police subjects: Theory and practice. Springfield, IL: Charles C. Thomas Publishers.

International Fire Service Training Association. (1981). Fire Service Instructor. Stillwater, OK: Oklahoma State University.

LAWS ASSOCIATED WITH LEARNING

It is commonly accepted in the field of education that there are "laws of learning". They were developed by E.L. Thorndike to explain in a general way why people react or behave in certain ways in their learning experiences.

Law of Readiness

Students tend to learn best when they are ready for learning. People who are going to learn anything will need to be physically and emotionally ready. The first step for an instructor is to motivate the students. Then it is important to keep them interested. Readiness is maintained by breaks and alterations the learning experience. This helps to avoid the "Learning Plateaus" in which learning becomes more difficult because the learner has grown tired or the material has lost its attraction.

Law of Exercise

Repetition is the basic element of learning. Skills are learned by practice. the best learning is based on activity which involves the mind and the body. Repetition is not useful unless the student can see meaning behind the repetition.

Law of Effect

People will be attracted to those concepts and activities which provide some reward or a sense of satisfaction. Praise or blame can be an effective learning tool if used properly. Rewards, however, have the greater power to positively effect learning because they build a positive sense of security, belonging, self esteem and self actualization (Maslow, 1954).

Law of Association

The mind will compare new information with information which is already known. Therefore it is easier to learn new information if it can be associated to past experience.

Law of Primacy

The first experience in any activity is of paramount importance. Make sure that whatever is being taught is accurate and complete. First impressions count more than we realize. Incomplete or inaccurate information sets up learning which can be difficult to unlearn and relearn later.

Law of Recency

The more recent the practice of skills the better will be the performance of those skills when they are needed. For example, reminding oneself of the steps in a CISD just before providing one will help the team to perform better.

Law of Intensity

People will have the best recall of those things which are quite vivid. Threatening, frightening, disgusting, painful and exceedingly joyful experiences are usually remembered.
(IFSTA, 1981; Bachtler, 1989)

CISM / CISD COURSE DEVELOPMENT

Developing a CISM, a crisis intervention course or a CISD course is not one of the easiest tasks in life, but there are rewards for preparing people to provide services to others or possibly even to save their own careers or health. In the chapters to follow several courses have been developed for the benefit of CISM or CISD team instructors. They can easily be used as models for the instructor who must develop a crisis or stress course or any human elements course. There are many issues which must be considered as one begins the task of course development. If some general ideas are kept in mind course development will be much easier.

For example it is important to know from the outset:

- Type of information to be presented
- Quantity of information to be presented
- The level of complexity of information to be presented.

Once a course idea had been generated and the initial reviews are completed and there is administrative approval to continue course development, then the course developer prepares an analysis of what is to be achieved by the course. The next step is to develop information about the target population who will be taught the information. Next the instructor needs to develop an understanding of the instructional requirements. How many instructors will it take to train the personnel? What support services will they need? What audiovisual support will need to be developed? What materials are readily available? How will the new course affect the training schedule for the organization? What is the estimated cost of the instruction? What facilities will be required? etc.

The *last steps* of course development include these:

- Obtain necessary technical assistance
- Write course objectives

- Write student performance objectives

- Write enabling objectives

- Develop a specific instructor guide for the course

- Develop student materials

- Develop or purchase audiovisual aids

- Develop evaluation criteria

- Pilot test the program

- Revise program as necessary

- Implement / monitor / revise / maintain
  (Harrison, 1977; IFSTA, 1981; GP Courseware, 1983; Fay, 1988
  Bachtler, 1989; Walz, 1990)

PLANNING

Planning seems to be the area of the educational / instructional professions which gets the most complaints from teachers and instructors. Many say it is tedious and time consuming. It may be so for many, but the importance of individual instructor pre-planning cannot be overemphasized. The greatest number of failures in education and training will most likely be traced back to poor planning. Students, especially adult students know when an instructor is unprepared for class and they are angered by the apparent lack of care the instructor demonstrates toward them. In addition, unprepared instructors have a greater chance of making content errors in the classroom which can be difficult to repair later.

Each lesson should be carefully planned out by the instructor. Technically, if something happened to prevent the primary instructor from teaching a course segment, a secondary instructor should be able to enter the situation and teach the segment based on the lesson plan worked out by the primary instructor.

A lesson plan should include:

- Course title
- Lesson number
- Topic of the lesson
- Level of instruction
- Reference materials
- Audiovisual aids and equipment list
- Estimated teaching time required
- Performance objectives
- Enabling objectives
- The body of the lesson

> INTRODUCTION
>
> PRESENTATION
>
> APPLICATION
>
> EVALUATION

- Lesson overview
- Specific teaching points
- Summary points
- Class assignments
- Lead-in for next lesson
- Suggested instructional methods
- Instructor notes

(IFSTA, 1981; GP Courseware, 1983; Fay, 1988; Bachtler, 1989; Walz, 1990)

OBJECTIVES

This text would be incomplete if more information on objectives is not given. They are vital to both the planning and delivery aspects of instruction and deserve special note. As noted above there are three types of objectives. They are:

COURSE OBJECTIVES

PERFORMANCE OBJECTIVES

ENABLING OBJECTIVES

Course objectives are written in broad terms. These objectives are written to give the instructor and the student a "big picture" of the course. The conditions or criteria for measuring the success of the instruction are usually left out. Only the general behaviors are stated.

Example: At the conclusion of this course the student will be able to demonstrate knowledge of the functions and responsibilities of a CISM team.

Performance objectives are often called lesson objectives. The are far more specific than the course objectives and they clearly state not only the expected behavior, but also the conditions under which the behaviors should occur and the criteria by which those behaviors will be evaluated. Performance objectives are written with the goals of a specific lesson in mind.

Example: At the conclusion of this lesson the participant will be able to demonstrate the ability to properly intervene on the scene as a peer by correctly answering instructor questions and by describing how they would apply specific on scene support services (stabilization, nourishing, active listening, resource mobilization, etc.) to their fellow emergency workers.

Enabling objectives are highly specific. There are usually more of them and they are usually linked together for a student to reach a performance objective. Enabling objectives describe the performance expected. They may or may not include the criteria of measurement since these were covered in the Performance objective (lesson objective).

Example: Given a diagram of the seven phase debriefing process the student will be able to correctly name, in order, the phases of the debriefing and will be able to trace the course of the debriefing though the phases.

Objectives help the instructor and the student to organize their approach to the course and to specific lessons. Objectives help in the motivation process. They state why certain pieces of information are important and they clarify how the smaller pieces of information fit into the overall course. The objectives give the instructors and students direction in applying the information obtained in individual lessons and in the overall course.

FOUR STEP METHOD OF INSTRUCTION

Since most emergency services instructors are familiar with the four step method of instruction (preparation, presentation, application and evaluation) which is suggested in many of their training texts, the same method of instruction will be utilized in the basic CISD course outline later in this book. The four step method will be outlined and summarized in the following paragraphs in order to acquaint those who are unfamiliar with the process. The steps are interlocked with one another and should not be thought of separately although they will be discussed separately below. The separation is only to enhance the explanations.

PREPARATION - LEVEL ONE

Without the proper preparation of both the instructor and the students, effective learning is a near impossibility. It is important that the student be motivated to learn and that the lesson be mapped out in advance for the student. The lessen objectives must be laid out for the students. The instructor also attempts to arouse curiosity and interest in the students. Motivation of the student is one of the primary activities of the preparation segment.

PRESENTATION - LEVEL TWO

In the presentation step the instruction is given. New concepts are suggested to the learners. New information is presented and teaching aids are employed. Demonstration of the skills associated with the learning are provided. Questions can be asked and feedback given during the presentation.

APPLICATION - LEVEL THREE

The application step in the instructional method allows for the student to try out the new concepts and skills which have been taught. Problem solving strategies and skills performance are expected in this step. Asking a student to explain the key steps in the performance is typical during this step. This is an excellent time to correct errors.

EVALUATION - LEVEL FOUR

In this step the instructor attempts to determine if the instruction has been adequate and if the learning has occurred. The learner attempts to apply the concepts and skills with little or no direct supervision from the instructor. Questioning and skills demonstration are the usual methods associated with the evaluation step in the four step process.

When the levels of learning are presented in the course outline later in this book the implication is that one or more levels of learning is being emphasized. All levels are present in each student-instructor contact but, in some lessons, the emphasis is only on one, two or three levels.

The brief outline of the four step method was presented for convenience only. Remember, it is not the purpose of this book to teach people how to instruct. Instructional knowledge and skills are presumed if an individual is going to instruct others in CISM / CISD or related topics.

CONCLUSION

This chapter covered the essential components of instruction and learning especially as it relates to the instruction of *human elements* information by CISM or CISD teams. The reader was given an overview of the instructional process and the duty of emergency organizations to provide human elements training. In addition, the chapter covered a strategy for human elements training for the adult learner and the basic elements of learning. The chapter also contains information on the laws of learning, the domains of learning and course development and lesson planning. The chapter concluded with a description of the four step process of instruction which will be utilized in other chapters later in this book.

Note: Gratitude is expressed to Bruce Walz, Ed.D., Assistant Professor of Emergency Health Services at the University of Maryland, who reviewed the chapter and made many useful suggestions which have been incorporated into the text.

CHAPTER 4

Instructional Methods in Human Elements Training

INTRODUCTION

Material in the affective domain is considered by many the most difficult to teach and, by far, the most difficult to learn. A fair share of the content of crisis programs, stress programs and CISD training courses is directly in the affective domain. It is not that the methods of teaching are so radically different. They are not. What is different is that there is a greater degree of psychological reactions which occur during CISM or CISD courses. These reactions occur in the students and, at times, in the instructor often times by virtue of the work histories they bring to the training. Instructors need to be alert to the subtle changes which take place in the group of students and recognize when course content or process is producing distressing reactions.

It will be necessary, on occasion, to temporarily stop or divert the class to assist an individual who is experiencing considerable distress as a result of the memories of past events which come to mind as the instructor presents crisis or stress related material. Many students approach the instructor at breaks or in between sessions to discuss the psychological discomfort they are encountering. Brief peer counseling sessions are sometimes necessary. That is one reason why it is highly recommended that emergency services instructors have peer counseling training before they begin to instruct in the human elements of the crisis and stress fields.

This chapter will be helpful to crisis and stress instructors in the actual delivery of the information in their courses. It contains detailed information on lecturing, audiovisual supported lectures, role playing, guest lecturers, discussions and skills instruction and demonstration. One of the most important aspects of the chapter is that it provides cautions for instructors to remember when they are present-ing crisis and stress related topics to emergency providers and disaster workers.

METHODS OF INSTRUCTION

There are many ways to educate and train people. Some methods work very well in virtually any circumstance. Others are effective in a limited number of situations. For some instructional methods there are inherent risks which should be considered before the techniques are chosen. The following paragraphs will explore some of the advantages and disadvantages associated with various methods of instruction. There are five basic types of instruction which are commonly referred to in textbooks on education. They are:

- Lecture
- Illustrated lecture
- Guided discussion
- Demonstration
- Skills instruction

LECTURE

The lecture method is a common and traditional form of instruc-tion. When presented by a knowledgeable and skilled instructor, the lecture can be interesting and exciting. It can enhance the student's knowledge of stress or crisis (or any other topic). Lectures permit a rapid presentation of information. They are also useful when there is a large volume of information to teach and a limited time in which to teach it. They are ideal for large groups. They are easy to plan and have very little development cost. Preparation, planning and an enthusiastic and skillful delivery are essential in the lecture format of instruction. A major advantage is that the lecture requires little or no equipment to deliver the information.

There are some disadvantages to a lecture format. A poorly

planned and badly delivered lecture has the potential to ruin the crisis or stress topic for the listener. Excessive lecturing is difficult to do. It tires the lecturer and may bore the students. It is very difficult to judge the student's grasp of the information if lecture is the primary instructional method. There is little opportunity for student feedback to the instructor. Lectures were not designed with student participation in mind. Strict lecture usually produces a situation in which there is limited retention on the part of the students. Lecture is the weakest method to teach manual skills.

In spite of its weaknesses, lecture, the art of communicating information verbally to another person, remains an important tool in instruction. It should be used effectively and delivered in an expert and lively manner whenever it is employed (Harrison, 1977; IFSTA. 1981; GP Courseware, 1983; Fay, 1988; Bachtler, 1988; Walz, 1990).

ILLUSTRATED LECTURE

One of the very best learning formats is the illustrated lecture. In this teaching method the instructor uses his or her voice to explain points which may be projected onto a screen by slides or overhead transparencies. These visual aids are called "projectable aids". Some people call this the "audiovisual supported lecture". The graphics are two dimensional and may include non projectable learning aids such as blackboards, flip charts and handouts. Other audio-visual formats such as audio tapes and video tapes can be added into this type of lecture, but those techniques will be addressed separately in the sections to follow.

The student clearly benefits because there are two senses involved - hearing and seeing. This intensifies the learning and increases the chance that students will retain what they learn . Students are more interested by information which is delivered by means of two or more senses (IFSTA, 1981).

There are some distinct disadvantages to the illustrated lecture. One of the most common problems with this teaching method is the over reliance of an instructor on one or more types of audiovisual support. If there is an equipment failure, the instructor may not be able to continue the lecture without the aid of the audiovisuals. Well prepared instructors always prepare extra lecture material or some other class activity - just in case. Poorly prepared instructors sometimes try to cover their lack of preparation by excessively relying on audio visual support. Students generally recognize this weakness and they lose interest in the topic because they do not perceive interest in the topic on the part of the instructor.

Some instructors falsely believe that audiovisuals will enable them to go to class with less preparation. The opposite is actually true. It takes more preparation to make sure that the audiovisuals fit smoothly into the overall presentation. It is also very important that the audio visuals be carefully designed. Unreadable slides or transparencies crammed with too much information make it more difficult to learn the material which is being presented.

Equipment to project the slides and transparencies is frequently bulky and transportation of the equipment complicates the process of instruction outside of an instructor's home base. The potential to damage slides and transparencies is ever present and instructors should be ready with alternate plans if something is damaged or unworkable.

One final note on the illustrated lecture is the fact that audiovisual support is frequently expensive. Equipment to project the images is certainly not cheap and the slides and transparencies can be costly to develop (Harrison, 1977; IFSTA, 1981; GP Courseware, 1983; Fay; 1988, Bachtler, 1988; Walz, 1990).

GUIDED DISCUSSION

A guided discussion provides a great deal of interaction between the instructor and the students. While the instructor verbally imparts information, there is a great deal of questioning of the students to obtain their feedback. A key to success is ability of the instructor to choose the right "seed" questions to stimulate the discussion. It is very common in adult education programs. It is especially useful when it is used as a problem solving method. It helps the learner to internalize the information being discussed because they have such active involvement in the information as it is presented. Discussions are particularly useful in determining if the student has learned the material. If they have, they will be able to readily answer the questions asked by the instructor (Warren, 1964; Neff and Weimer, 1989).

The problems encountered in guided discussion sometimes cause classroom instructors to limit their use of the technique. It is a time consuming process not designed for the teaching of a great deal of information. It is often difficult to control the discussion and guided discussions frequently drift away from the course and lesson objectives. Discussions need careful planning of the questions which are going to be used by the instructor. The guided discussion requires a very thorough knowledge of the subject matter on the part of the instructor. (Bachtler, 1988).

DEMONSTRATION

The demonstration entails learning by seeing someone else exhibit a skill. It is accompanied by verbal information, commentary and instructions. Besides illustrated lecture, demonstrations are the second most utilized method of instruction for instructors teaching stress or crisis concepts. It enhances the learning experience and shows that the process being demonstrated actually works. Students who view demonstrations have a far better perception of the material being taught then they would have by lecture alone or by illustrated lecture.

There are some distinct disadvantages to the demonstration. It takes a good deal of planning time. It is not only time consuming in the preparation stage, it is time consuming in its delivery and in its follow up. Some teaching points can be easily missed in the demonstration unless special care is made to focus on those points. Visibility may be a problem for some students and they may not see the same portions of the demonstration because they are seeing them from different angles. The physical aspects of the teaching area will have much to do with the learning which takes place. If people can not hear or see the instructor, they will not be able to learn.

If a serious mistake is made in a demonstration, it should be stopped and an explanation of the problem should be given to the students. The demonstration can be backed up and restarted at some convenient point to assure that the mistake can be corrected.

The demonstration is usually followed by a question and answer period involving the instructor and all of the students so that all may benefit from clarifications and answers to the questions. A summary of key points should be made before the students are released or before the class moves onto the next lesson.

More will be said regarding demonstration when the role play is described later in this chapter (IFSTA, 1981; Bachtler, 1988)

SKILLS INSTRUCTION

Skills instruction is not truly a distinct teaching method. It is more an extension of the demonstration. Except in the case of the skills instruction, the students are the prime participants and the instructor observes and provides guidance and direction. The instructor has to be particularly alert because the students, who may be trying out skills for the first time are likely to make mistakes. They will need careful and considerate correction for the mistakes which do not embarrass them, but instead accepts and praises what they do correctly and moves them onto better performances with each correction. Skills develop in a stepped fashion. The steps of skill building are:

- Observe and mentally rehearse
- Perform activity according to instruction
- Develop accuracy and precision
- Establish smooth sequences and actions
- Develop proficiency with no wasted motion

Skills instruction is more difficult than the demonstration because the instructor has to step aside and let the students handle the activity. It is also difficult from the point of view of the instructor because the instructor must view all of the students and control the session simultaneously. The skills instruction session has some of the same problems as the demonstration method of instruction. One of the key problems besides those mentioned above is the fact that it is time consuming. Another problem is that students who are worried about their own performance may not be able to see and hear what others are doing and they might miss some important teaching points.

When carefully planned and monitored the skills instruction method can enhance student learning. Although more difficult for the instructor, especially when applied to the type of training in crisis and stress courses, it is a very effective and memorable way to learn (Bachtler, 1988).

SPECIAL INSTRUCTIONAL AIDS AND TECHNIQUES

Video tapes

Well organized and professionally developed video programs can be extremely productive in teaching human elements topics to emergency personnel. The audiovisual combination on the video tape format provides many of the basic elements necessary for effective learning. The use of video tapes is another form of the illustrated lecture except the instructor provides information before and after the video tape and allows the video tape to present some of the information in between the instructor's involvement. As pointed out earlier, people learn better when more than one sense in involved in the learning process (IFSTA, 1981).

A drawback to the use of video taped programs occurs when the instructor sets up a video for the students and disappears from the classroom without any intention of furthering a discussion after the video tape ends. The students may learn something from the video tape, but they are deprived of the benefits of the intensified learning which can take place when the instructor leads a discussion or allows a question and answer period. The best use of the guided discussion method of instruction for crisis and stress training, in the experience of the authors, is when it is applied after the students view a video taped program.

Hand out material

There are basically three types of handouts which are used in human elements programs. The first is the type which contains important information which the instructor expects the students to save as useful reference material for future use. The second type of hand out material is information which the instructor thinks students might find interesting or useful, but it is not vital to the understanding of the course material. Both of these handouts are usually given out with the intention that the student will take the material away from the class and read it at home. Instructors usually find it helpful to either give out such material well before the class begins or at the end of the class. Otherwise students tend to look at this material while the instructor is trying to cover other points. Occasionally, students might make noise with the papers and distract one another.

The third type of handout material is the type which is going to be used during the lesson. Usually the information on such a handout is important enough for each student to have their own copy. For example, charts and diagrams or a worksheet or a stress test may be an integral part of the lecture. This type of hand out is distributed at the time it is needed in the lesson. In many cases, a handout of this nature is repeatedly referred to during the remainder of the presentation.

Hand out material can be very helpful in clarifying the main points of a presentation and in recalling important information long after the lecture is completed. It is important to assure that hand outs enhance the learning. They should be limited in scope. That is, handout material for human elements classes should avoid the extremes of providing too much or too little information. In addition, they should be well organized, clearly printed, concise, visually attractive and interesting (IFSTA,. 1981; Bachtler, 1988; Walz, 1990).

Role plays

Role playing means that the class participants engage in an interactive learning experience with each other under the direction of the instructor. In this instructional format, class participants are given roles to act out in the role play (Warren, 1964). This learning experience can be a powerful, unforgettable lesson. It can teach by practice things which could not easily be taught in a strict lecture even with a very skillful lecturer. Role playing is especially useful when teaching in the affective domain (Bachtler, 1988).

Before jumping on the role play bandwagon, however, instructors are advised to consider a number of important issues. Role playing is not an easy classroom task and it certainly can be a very time consuming one if it is done properly.

The first issue of importance in role playing is that emergency personnel frequently express dislike for the process if it exposes their feelings or other private issues. Role plays can stir uncomfortable emotions and emergency personnel do not like to let these feelings out before their fellow workers. They fear that those emotions will be used against them, or that they might be embarrassed or possibly incapacitated by their own hidden feelings when they are brought to the surface.

Another problem which might be encountered in the use of role plays is that they can become quite realistic and intense to the people who are participating in them. Role players may develop considerable psychological discomfort during the experience and the instructor may need to stop the role or alter its course. Frequently, those who may be distressed by the experience will need some support from the instructor after it is over to assist them in recovering emotionally from the experience.

The very best role playing situations will be:

• Well planned

- Carefully organized

- Within reasonable limits of time

- In accordance with the needs of the group

- With well briefed role players

- Time limited

- Discussed at their conclusion

- Provided with a signal for emergency stopping

- Planned to avoid recent local painful events

- Planned to avoid highly charged emotions

- Led by an instructor who is well trained

- Led by an instructor who is willing to help those who are stuck on painful emotions or when they are feeling lost and vulnerable

When used carefully and by a good instructor, role playing can be an enormously helpful learning tool. If, on the other hand it is applied badly, it has the potential to produce emotional pain for a role player who has experienced a traumatic event in their past and who is not yet ready to deal with the emotions which are generated in the role play.

Case Reviews

Case reviews entail the presentation by a class member of a case or situation in which the individual had direct personal involvement. The class may provide feedback in the form of ideas, suggestions, reactions or feelings. They might also ask questions for clarification or elaboration (Bachtler, 1988).

Instructors guide the discussion along, answer some of the questions, provide feedback , ask additional guiding questions and generally monitor the group. It is important to insure that no one person dominates the discussion and that no one who wishes to participate is unable to get his or her points across to the other class members.

In this educational format, it is very important not to put the students "on the spot". The assumption has to be made that if a student declines an invitation to speak during the session, they probably have their own good reasons for their refusal. When an instructor is teaching stress, crisis or any material associated with an individual's emotional life, the right of refusal to participate in a discussion should always be respected.

Guest Lecturer

Many stress and crisis courses can benefit significantly from guest lecturers. Some instructors utilize experts in the field while others use personnel who have survived traumatic events. There are cautions which should be considered if either type of guest lecturer is chosen.

If the guest lecturer is not prepared to deal with the emergency services "culture", the task of speaking to such groups can be a difficult one. Guest lecturers who cannot adapt to the emergency personnel may produce a loss of credibility.

Here are some guidelines for using guest lecturers in the Crisis or stress course:

- Invite guests who can contribute to the course content
- Bring in guests with expertise the instructor lacks
- Ask guests with different backgrounds and views
- Arrange for guests well in advance
- Provide guests with suggestions about what they might cover in the class
- Provide guests with background of course / students
- Announce the guests before they arrive
- Give students background on the guest

- Introduce the guests
- Sometimes co-presenting is helpful in learning
- Relate the guest's material to remainder of course
- Avoid giving students impression that anyone can be a guest lecturer
- Do not have guests only when instructor is away from class
- Do not invite guests unless the quality and style of their presentation is known in advance (Weimer, 1991)

The guest lecturer who has survived a traumatic event presents a different kind of challenge to the instructor. The instructor should be very cautious in choosing the "survivor" type of guest lecturer. Care must be taken to assure that the person has sufficiently recovered from the traumatic event and that the presentation is not going to produce psychological or physical harm to the traumatized person. Since the "survivor" is in a relatively vulnerable position when they are talking about their emotional trauma, a separate section has been developed below to guide the instructor in choosing and utilizing a "survivor" guest instructor.

The Survivor's Story

Inviting a guest speaker who has survived a major traumatic event can add substantially to the quality of a course on crisis or stress. Survivors describe interesting stories from which much can be learned. These types of guest lecturers add a factor of intense drama to the learning environment. Great caution is urged about over enthusiasm about the survivor type guest presentation. There is no doubt that much can be learned from those who have survived critical incidents. However, several important considerations should be addressed before decisions are made to arrange for such a speaker.

Probably the most important issue to be considered is the well being of the guest lecturer who has survived a critical incident. The instructor should find out if the person is sufficiently recovered from the event to be able to speak publicly about it. A person who made it through a critical incident should not be expected to endure further hardship just to make a presentation on their experience. Before the person is committed to speaking, the instructor should have a frank discussion with the potential presenter about how ready the person is to discuss their experience to a group.

Some people are able to talk about a bad experience with family members or with very close friends, but they feel too uncomfortable discussing their painful experiences with strangers. This feeling should be respected and no one should be pressured to speak. Other survivors would be able to present their experience by means of video tape or audio tape, but not live in a classroom. Decisions not to discuss an event or to limit one's discussion only to a taped interview should be respected. If there is significant doubt that a person is ready to present his or her experience, then the request for the presentation should be at least temporarily delayed until the circumstances improve.

Those who agree to tell their stories should be advised that they may withhold any aspects of the story which are too uncomfortable to bring out. Many people feel obligated to tell everything when faced with an audience, a microphone or a camera. It is important for them to know that they have a right to refuse to disclose anything which causes them excessive pain or which is too personal.

People who do agree to relate their experiences before an audience should be told who is going to be in the audience and what points the instructor would most like to be addressed. This helps to avoid situations in which the presenter emphasizes concepts or aspects of the experience which would not necessarily add to the group's learning about the topic. It also avoids inadvertent disclosure of tactical information which should not be disclosed to a general audience.

A decision needs to be reached before the presentation about whether questions will be allowed or not. If there is any discomfort about the possibility of questions, the class should be told that questions will not be allowed.

Sometimes it is helpful for a potential guest lecturer to have a practice run before video cameras or a small trusted audience before a survivor presents before the real audience. this can help to improve the person's self confidence and the delivery. Remember, just because a person survives a traumatic event does not mean they automatically become an excellent public speaker.

If a survivor is still in therapy to help resolve the harmful effects of a significant stress, it would be wise to encourage the survivor to check out the idea of a presentation with the therapist. This will assist the person in avoiding a potentially harmful situation. Public speaking about one's experience can be very therapeutic. But, there is potential that it could also be harmful if the conditions are not right.

Instructors should never have a survivor present without a proper introduction to the students and a follow up discussion once the guest has completed the presentation. It is important to avoid presentations which are given only for "shock value", but which have no educational advantage. Excessive reliance on the survivor presentation without other forms of stress education should be avoided.

STUDENT REACTIONS

Students in a stress class or other human elements may, at times, react very strongly to the material which is presented especially if it is graphic. They may react to the lecture material, to a guest lecturer or to a survivor's experience. Their reactions can be many and varied. They may become more subdued, abruptly leave the room and or show signs of anxiety, denial or anger. They might also react by discussing powerful events which have happened in their own lives. Although younger, less experienced emergency personnel are more likely to discuss the stress they felt as result of a call, it is not uncommon for older, well experienced personnel to have painful memories of past events which they may wish to discuss with the instructor.

Instructors should be alert to the potential reactions in their students and they should be prepared to assist students who react to their own distress which arises as they view or hear crisis and stress related material. Assistance to students may take on many forms.

Some self disclosure by one or more students is to be expected. In fact, when it occurs, it should be generally accepted, encouraged and supported. Talking about personally painful material can be of great benefit to most students. It helps to bring up material which might never have been disclosed if the stress class had not been presented. Opening up stored, painful material frequently relieves emotional pressure and frees a person to use his or her energies in a far more productive manner. They no longer have to waste energy trying to constantly suppress these painful experiences.

When students open up in class, it is generally a good idea to listen to them carefully as they discuss their stressful experiences. Encourage further discussion if it appears to be appropriate. Many students have trouble opening up before a group so they wait until a break in the class or until the class is finished and approach the instructor individually. This in itself is an indication of the intensity of the event. The more powerful an impact an event has had, the more likely a disclosure will either not occur or will only occur in private.

The first step in helping a student balance the stressful experience he or she wishes to discuss is to listen very carefully to the story. Avoid the temptation to jump to conclusions before the student finishes. Also, be careful not to make efforts to give advice too early. This can be especially harmful if it occurs in the midst of the story. Instead, listen, acknowledge and validate the emotional content and suggest a limited amount of advice only as part of a natural conversation in which the student draws his or her own conclusions. Many people just need some good listening or a little reassurance that they handled the event adequately.

Although self disclosure is useful and helpful process for a distressed student, there are times when it may be counter productive. For instance, if it appears that the disclosure is producing more harm than good, it needs to be gently modified or gently stopped or postponed by the instructor.

Here are some signs an instructor might look for which suggest that the disclosure from a student might be harmful to the student or possibly to the class:

- Information brought up by the student in class is extremely personal and would be better discussed with the instructor or with a mental health professional in private. Examples would include information about personal sexual practices or preferences, personal drug or alcohol abuse, criminal behaviors, etc.

- The student shows extreme psychological distress during the discussion. The distress the student exhibits is far beyond the usual reactions such as trembling hands, tears and shaky voice, which would be expected. Instead the student may become hysterical, panic struck, and demonstrate significant loss of emotional control, excessive anger and rage or extreme depression

- Suicidal thinking is present. When this occurs, the instructor must refer the student for immediate psychological evaluation. Every effort must be made to assure that the student actually seeks out the recommended professional help.

- Symptoms of active psychosis are present. Immediate referral to an emergency department at a general hospital or psychiatric clinic for psychological evaluation is indicated.

- A history of child abuse or incest is described by the student. This person should be encouraged to pursue professional assistance.

- A student begins to describe a classmate's stress reactions or personal behaviors. The person described may be in the group at the time or could be well known to the group. The student who is bringing up such material should be immediately stopped. The classroom is no place for such discussions. If the student who brings up the topic is expressing concern for the person who is being described and is really trying to find a way to help that person, the instructor should suggest that the concerned student see the instructor after the class. The class should be reminded that they may discuss their own personal experiences, but should avoid discussing other students or people well known to the students in the class.

Whenever an instructor is listening to the personal stories of distressed students, it is wise to keep a few basic ground rules in mind. These help to prevent problems and misunderstandings. First, advice giving should be kept to a minimum and should always be given cautiously. Next, get the whole story before suggesting anything. All supportive comments or the minimal amount of advice which is given needs to be well thought out. Whatever advice is given should be practical, realistic, reasonable and prudent. The best advice is that which is of a general nature and which would more than likely be given to any other person who might be in a similar situation. Instructors should stick to material which is well documented as typical advice for the situation the student is in.

It not uncommon for human elements instructors to advise one or more students to seek out professional assistance. It is helpful if the instructor knows of a few mental health professionals in the community who have experience with emergency personnel. An instructor who is caught off guard by a student's request for or need for professional assistance can usually rely on the psychiatry department of a hospital or on a crisis clinic for a referral resource list.

CONFIDENTIALITY

Once a student discloses personal information to an instructor, that information must be held in absolute confidence. Breaking confidentiality is always destructive and it can cause significant harm for anyone involved. Students generally place a high level of trust on their instructors and they are devastated when they feel betrayed. The instructor who is willing to listen to personal information must also have a willingness to keep confidential all aspects of the discussion.

The only legitimate breaking of confidentiality occurs when the person has disclosed information which indicates that he or she or another person is in clear and imminent danger or when some other legal or ethical principle dictates such disclosure. Under these highly unusual circumstances, confidentiality may need to be broken for a greater good.

GENERAL CAUTIONS IN TEACHING HUMAN ELEMENTS

The sections above should point out that teaching crisis and stress related topics is not a simple task. It takes care, planning, interest in the topic areas and a high degree of professionalism on the part of the instructor. A few additional cautions might be helpful. They will be outlined in the paragraphs below.

Balance is the key concept in teaching human elements, especially when the audience is emergency personnel. Instructors sometimes have a tendency to try to fit too much into a presentation. Students are limited in the amounts of information they are able to absorb. Avoid overloading a presentation. There is a tremendous amount of information to be presented in the human elements field. It cannot be taught in one session.

The other side of the balance, of course, is to avoid teaching too little. Human elements training deserves more than just a half hour of a course which includes a hundred hours or more on other topics. Remember, emergency workers have a right to know about crisis and stress and its effects on their work and their families. Instructors should not, therefore, cut short their presentation on human elements or just give out a few handouts on stress in order to use the time to cover other topics in the curriculum. They should, instead, plan to use the allotted time to teach enough human elements information so that the students will have a working knowledge of the topic sufficient to help them survive stressful job experiences.

Some instructors in the stress field like to stimulate their students by presenting audiovisual tapes or by telling stories of horrible events just for the shock value and not for any educational value. They often present the material without appropriate links to the topic of the presentation. They also take little or no time to explain the cases in a manner that would point out beneficial lessons which could be learned from those situations.

Some events can be presented to enhance stress programs. They should be carefully presented and adequately discussed. Showing a video with disturbing scenes without warning people that they are about to see some distressing sights can be harmful to the members of the audience. This is especially so if a student has had a recent similarly disturbing experience in the field.

It is far better to warn people that something in a audio tape or a video tape is potentially disturbing. This allows an individual to make a decision to leave the room if they perceive that the material might be too much for them at that time in their life. Most emergency workers will sit through a video despite its content. They do appreciate the warning because the warning helps to cut their stress by giving them the ability to mentally prepare to manage distressing sights and sounds.

The guidelines which follow will help the instructor to properly present the graphic audiovisual material which may enhance the affective domain of learning.

- Be certain that the case to be presented by audiovisuals has educational value for the course. Ask yourself if the material will greatly enhance specific points in the presentation.

- Warn students that the audiovisuals to follow contain graphic descriptions of traumatic events

- Provide an adequate introduction to the audiovisual material to be presented.

- Allow adequate time after the presentation to discuss the program. Efforts should be made to relate the audiovisual material with specific learning points in the overall presentation. Discuss the distress which may have been generated by the presentation.

- Instructors should be prepared to assist any student who might have encountered distress as a result of exposure to the audiovisual program.

CONCLUSION

This chapter provided detailed information of specific methods of teaching human elements related topics. The five major instructional methods (lecture, illustrated lecture, guided discussion, demonstration, and skills instruction) were described and the uses of those methods in teaching crisis and stress topics was mentioned. The chapter also discussed special instructional techniques such as video tapes, handouts and role playing. Special instructions were given on how to manage the presentation of a survivor's story.

A very important portion of the chapter is the section on possible student reactions to the traumatic material presented in the class. The instructor role in identifying and assisting distressed students was described. Instructors were given guidelines to use when faced with a distressed student. It was clearly stated, for example that an instructor has an obligation to keep confidential any personal information a student brings out in private conversation unless ethical or legal mandates disallow confidentiality. Other cautions about teaching crisis intervention and stress related topics were presented in the latter sections of the chapter.

The next chapter will provide course outlines to assist the instructor in course development. The next chapter also contains suggestions on course presentation and also on continuing education (in-service education).

CHAPTER 5

Course Outlines For Teaching Crisis Intervention, General Stress Management, Critical Incident Stress and Command Stress Courses

INTRODUCTION

Structuring a new course in a relatively new field can often be a difficult, if not overwhelming, task . Instructors may not be sure of what has already been accomplished and what still needs to be done. The guidelines are either sparse or non existent. The literature may still be in an early stage of development. A standardized course outline is initially difficult to develop in a new field because the priorities for training are changing rapidly. For example, in the early seventies, emergency medical courses at all levels struggled to teach people better bandaging and splinting techniques. But, by the end of that decade, the emphasis had switched to other areas including the use of anti shock trousers and esophageal obturator airways. And in the eighties the emphasis shifted again to providing emergency personnel with basic human elements training programs such as crisis intervention and stress management.

The field of human elements training has seen its own changes over the last dozen years. In crisis intervention, for instance, the emphasis from the mid seventies into the early eighties was on "talk down" procedures for LSD drug users. Today the emphasis has dramatically changed to the issue of violence. Emergency personnel are being taught street survival tactics. In the field of stress studies, the early emphasis was on defining the problem called stress in the emergency services. The emphasis now is on prevention programs, family life programs, critical incident stress interventions and peer counselor support services. Emergency workers today no longer need programs which tell them how to define stress in their work and in their lives. They can define it themselves. Now they want to know more about preventing the stress problem and reducing it when it does occur.

Courses are likely to change over time. As developments are made in the field of human elements training, the emphasis in courses will need to change accordingly. It is, of course, much easier to make changes in courses if the instructors have a baseline from which to start. That is the purpose of this chapter. It will provide some core training course outlines which reflect the current state of the art in crisis and stress training. As the field changes, instructors may develop from these core courses, a variety of short or long courses for use with CISM teams or for use with operations personnel and command officers.

Some of the courses will be broad topical outlines only or simply suggestions as to which areas should be covered in a course. Other course outlines in this chapter will provide more details including course objectives and information on the length of the course and the format of the training. The courses presented in this chapter are designed to give only the basic skeleton on which an instructor could build the remainder of a course including detailed lesson plans and specific teaching points. This approach allows instructors to build in certain areas of emphasis which might be necessary for certain jurisdictions or in certain areas of the country. It is also important that they put specific lesson objectives into their own words to assure the material is covered in the manner in which the instructors will feel most comfortable.

The basic CISD course will be handled in the next chapter and will be the most detailed course outline of all. That chapter will provide detailed lesson plans for a basic CISD course with objectives and specific teaching points.

Developing a course is neither easy nor is it fast. It can be a difficult and time consuming process if it is done properly. In the affective areas of learning, which crisis and stress training involve to some degree, the development of courses can be even more difficult and frustrating. This chapter should be very helpful to instructors because it provides the rudiments of crisis and stress management course planning. It should save busy instructors some time as they develop human elements training programs for their departments.

Instructors should keep in mind the course development procedures which were described earlier in this book or referred to in other instructor textbooks. It is assumed for the sake of brevity in this chapter, that the administrative approval for the course has already been obtained. *So, the administrative approval aspects of course development are purposely omitted from this chapter.* Instructors should follow all appropriate course development steps including administrative review and approval when they are developing their own courses. The course development system in this book is only a general guideline and not comprehensive tool for course development.

CRISIS INTERVENTION COURSE OUTLINE

Crisis intervention is a broad field with many possible topics for inclusion in a course. Each of the topics can be taught individually or as part of an overall crisis course. Critical incident stress (CIS) is an example of a topic which is part of the overall crisis intervention field but which has received so much attention that it has been developed not only into a full course of its own, but into a series of courses. Typical topics in the crisis field will be presented in the next section of this chapter.

I. Crisis Intervention Course Overview

A. Idea: A short course to familiarize emergency personnel with the issue of crisis intervention and the need for special services for

victims of crises such as violence, drug abuse, sexual assault, alcohol intoxication, suicide, etc.

B. Description: A crisis intervention overview course is designed to give the learners a brief summary of crisis intervention. This course is designed in such a manner that the learner will not be able to develop specific skills because the course is too brief. The learners will, however, become familiar with core concepts of crisis intervention theory and practice.

C. Length of course: Between 1 and 3 hours. Little to nothing of value can be presented on this topic in less than one hour. In fact, in one hour only the most rudimentary of concepts can be presented. Three hours allows for greater detail in the presentation and the possibility of more questions asked by learners.

D. Format: The format for this course is either lecture or illustrated lecture in a classroom.

E. Technical assistance required? It is best to have the course reviewed by a mental health professional who is very familiar with the field of crisis intervention.

F. Course objectives: At the conclusion of the overview class in crisis intervention the participant will be able to:

1. Define the words crisis as a state of emotional turmoil and crisis intervention (CI) as a method of stabilizing the person or group and restoring them to as normal a function as possible.

2. Define maturational crisis and state the difference between maturational crisis and situational crisis.

3. List events which are commonly thought of as crises including suicide, sexual assault, violence, sudden death, child abuse, drug abuse, alcohol intoxication, family conflict, disasters, psychiatric disturbance, and severe stress.

4. Describe the steps in the crisis intervention process including

access, assessment, stabilization, stimulus reduction, quick plan, implementation, maintenance and restoration to function.

5. Identify circumstances in which the emergency person could perform basic crisis intervention techniques while awaiting the implementation of specialized assistance.

II. Course Outlines:

A. One Hour Program Outline:

1. Title: Crisis intervention principles and practices for emergency services: an overview

2. Topic: Basic concepts of crisis and crisis intervention (CI)

3. Levels of instruction: Usually preparation and presentation

4. References:

Mitchell, J.T. and Resnik, H.L.P. (1981;1986). Emergency Response to Crisis. Ellicott City, MD: Chevron Publishing Corporation

Hafen, B.Q. and Frandsen, K.J. (1985) Psychological Emergencies and Crisis Intervention: A comprehensive guide for emergency personnel. Englewood, CO: Morton Publishing Company.

5. Audio visuals: Possibly slide projector, overhead or flip chart (Discretion of instructor)

Outline:

Topics:	Time	Learning Domain	notes
Introduction	5 min.	cognitive	brief intro. of field
Define crisis, etc.	10 min.	cognitive	maturational / situational
Common crises	5 min.	cognitive	list crises by group

Define crisis intervention.	5 min.	cognitive	active / temporary
List parts of C.I.	5 min	cognitive	stabilize/ mobilize/ restore
Case examples	10 min.	affective	use 1 or two examples
Applying C.I.	10 min.	cognitive	apply CI to field situations
Benefits of C.I.	5 min.	cognitive	easy / effective
Question - answer	5 min	cognitive	clarify points

B. Two Hour Program

The two hour program is much like the program outlined above except for three things. The first is that there is more time for each of the topics and more specifics are addressed. For example, there is usually more reference to specific topics such as suicide, violence, sexual assault, substance abuse, etc. Second, the learner is provided with a few more suggestions on how to manage such issues under field conditions. The third difference is that brief mention may be made of the impact which crisis work has on the rescuer.

C. Three Hour Program

The three hour program is the point at which the instructor can present a much more beneficial program about crisis intervention. The following topical outline displays the topics which are usually covered in a three hour time block. The instructor may use the table like display which was used to outline the one hour session above or the course outline can be written in a vertical format. The remainder of the course is very much like the factors in the sections above.

1. Part one:

General crisis theory (1 hour and 15 minutes)

- nature of crisis

- maturational crises

- situational crises

- effects of crisis

a. on the individual

b. on the family or group

c. on the organization

- general psychological response to crisis

- signs and symptoms of crisis

a. cognitive

b. physical

c. emotional

d. behavioral

Break (15 minutes)

2. Part two:

General principles of crisis intervention (CI) (1 hour and 30 minutes)

- access

- assessment

- stabilization

- mobilization of resources

- immediate implementation

- aim toward restoration to function

- applying CI in the field

- benefits of CI

- case examples

- questions and answers

D. One day Program Outline:

The one day crisis intervention program has many things in common with the three hour program. There is one main advantage and that is that the full day gives the instructor a chance to cover all of the material as in the three hour program in the morning and then add to it the material printed in the section below. It should be noted that the course objectives stated above can be expanded to cover the additional material in this longer course. For example the course objectives (6 and 7) which follow are in addition to the first five printed above under roman numeral I.F.

At the conclusion of this course the student will be able to:

6. Identify the relationship between alcohol and substance abuse and greater levels of violence

7. Describe a quick assessment procedure for identifying a person at risk of suicide.

The longer the course and the more details it encompasses, the more course objectives may need to be written. The course can and should be broken into specific segments or lessons and each lesson should have its own performance objectives as previously pointed out.

1. **Morning session** is identical to the material in the outline for the three hour program above (sections C1 and C2).

2. **Afternoon session** is made up of the following segments
   Part one (1 hour and 15 minutes)
   - Alcohol and substance abuse crises
   - Violence
     - family
     - child abuse
     - sexual assault

- Break (15 minutes)

Part two (1 hour and 30 minutes)
- Suicide
  - assessment
  - general intervention principles
- Multi casualty incidents
- Questions and answers

E. Two Day Program Outline:

The two day time frame allows for a much wider range of topics and it also allows a more in depth coverage of the material. In the two day format the instructor can rely on the use of more audio visual support and the use of role plays.

1. **Idea:** A two day workshop to present the basic concepts of crisis intervention.

2. **Description:** This course is arranged so that the learner is exposed to a broad range of crisis intervention topics and skills. The two day course provides the learner with an opportunity to practice some of those skills in role play situations with fellow students.

3. **Length:** Two full days

4. **Format:** The course uses lecture, illustrated lecture, demonstration and discussion to cover the material. Role plays help the student to gain greater command of the subject matter.

5. **Technical Assistance:** The course is generally taught by a mental health professional.

6. **Course objectives:** (note: only a sample of the course objectives are presented here. Others are in the sections above. Instructors may add or subtract from these course objectives)

At the conclusion of this course the participant will be able to:

a. Describe basic crisis theory.

CRISIS INTERVENTION

b. Define crisis intervention and name its key components.

c. Identify various crises and categorize them into maturational or situational crises.

d. Demonstrate basic crisis intervention skills by means of participating in role plays in which crises are managed.

e. Describe a quick assessment technique for suicide intervention.

f. Define and describe a variety of crisis events and state the prescribed methods for managing such events.

7. **Lesson plans**: Specific lesson plans must be developed by individual instructors.

8. **Performance objectives**: These detailed lesson objectives must be developed by the instructors.

9. **Teaching points**: To be developed by the instructor. Only general topics will be presented in this section.

10. **Title**: Theory and Practice of Crisis Intervention: a two day workshop.

11. **Lesson number**: Instructors need to break this course into smaller lesson components. This will be at instructor discretion.

12. **Domain of learning**: Cognitive, affective, and some psychomotor depending on the specific lesson.

13. **Levels of instruction**: preparation, presentation application evaluation depending on the lesson being covered.

14. **References**: Mitchell and Resnik (1986); Hafen and Frandsen (1985)

15. **Audiovisual support**: slide projector or overhead projector, video tape player and monitor, audio cassette player, other at the discretion of the instructor.

16. **Outline**:

a. Day one morning

- Introduction

- Basic Crisis theory

  - nature of crisis

  - define crisis

  - maturational vs situational crises

  - causes of crisis

  - effects of crisis

    a. on individuals

    b. on families or groups

    c. on organization

  - general psychological response to crisis

  - signs and symptoms

    a. cognitive

    b. physical

    c. emotional

    d. behavioral

- Crisis intervention definition / explanation

- General principles of crisis intervention

  - access

  - assess

  - stabilization

  - mobilization of resources

  - immediate implementation

  - restore to function

CRISIS INTERVENTION

- applications to the field

- benefits of crisis intervention

- Mental disturbance

  a. anxiety state

  b. psychosis

  c. transient personality disorder

  d. depression

  e. post-traumatic stress disorder (PTSD)

- Human communications during crisis

Note: Instructors will need to take breaks when appropriate. The topical outline presented here only depicts the typical morning session on day one of a two day program. The breakdown into specific lessons and the use of audiovisual support is at the discretion of the instructor for all segments of this course.

b. Day one afternoon

- Role play(s) psychologically distressed person

  - discussion

- Appropriate video tape on alcoholism - if available

- Alcohol abuse

  - the problems

  - the interventions

- Substance abuse

  - assessment

  - interventions

- Questions and answers

c. Day two morning

CRISIS INTERVENTION

- Violence
- Violence role play (use <u>threat</u> of violence as opposed to actual violence in the role play)

  - discussion
- Family violence
- Child abuse
- Sexual assault
- Suicide

  - assessment

  - intent

  - lethality

  - plan

  - history in family

  - interventions

  - listening

  - validating

  - accepting feelings

  - finding alternatives
- Threat of suicide role play

  - discussion
- Questions and answers

d. Day two afternoon

- Death and dying
- Role play on one of the previous topics
- Multiple casualty incidents / disasters

- Stress in operations personnel

- Cumulative stress reactions

- Critical incident stress (traumatic stress)

- Questions and answers

F. Sixteen weeks

Only the topical outline for the sixteen week (3 hours per week) course will be presented here. The material in the sections above should be helpful in developing a full course program.

- lesson 1 - Introduction
    - Expectations
    - Requirements
    - Assignments
    - Rudiments of crisis theory
    - Terminology
- lesson 2 - Crisis Theory
    - Crisis intervention
- lesson 3 - Human communication skills
    - Assessment skills
    - Interviewing techniques
- lesson 4 - Mentally disturbed persons
    - Assessment
    - Interventions
- lesson 5 - Mental status examination

- Legal aspects of crisis intervention
- criteria for intervention
- confidentiality

- lesson 6 - Family crises
    - theory of family
    - experience indicates....
    - intervention with a distress family

- lesson 7 - Managing the psychological needs of pediatric cases

- lesson 8 - Alcohol intoxication
    - complications
    - management

- lesson 9 - Substance abuse
    - types
    - assessment
    - interventions

- lesson 10 - Violence
    - safety

- lesson 11- Sexual assault
    - victims needs
    - evidence maintenance

- lesson 12 - Child abuse
    - neglect
    - battering

- lesson 13 - Special problems

- elderly

- retarded

- lesson 14 - Suicide

  -assessment

  -interventions

- lesson 15 - Multiple casualty incidents

- lesson 16 - Stress in emergency work

GENERAL STRESS MANAGEMENT COURSE OUTLINE

Distinctions need to be made here between general stress, cumulative stress, critical incident stress and Post Traumatic Stress Disorder. Unfortunately, some people have blended these issues together. Perhaps the following chart will help to clarify the significant differences which exist between the various types of stress

TYPES OF STRESS			
General Stress	Cumulative Stress	Acute Traumatic Stress	Post Traumatic Stress Disorder
Everyone has this type of stress all the time - day and night. This form of stress usually resolves within a day or two.	Prolonged stress which builds up after time and can lead to adverse mental and/or physical consequences	Also called Critical Incident Stress. Produces considerable psychological distress. Normal reaction to abnormal event	Post Traumatic Stress Disorder. Severe distress produced only by severe psychological traumatization. Can produce lasting changes in person's life and work. Produced by unresolved Critical Incident Stress. Generally needs professional assistance.

A general stress management course is most associated with the general stress which everyone experiences which is depicted on the left hand side of the diagram, specifically daily and cumulative stress.

I. Overview course on general stress management

A. Idea: A course to cover the topic of common stress. It is a course that could be taught in modules and expanded or compressed as necessary to suit the needs of particular organizations. This course is envisioned as a general course that could be taught to recruit as well as in service education courses.

B. Description: General stress management is a course which can be provided in one hour, two hours, three hours one day or two days. The expansion in time allows for a greater range and depth of material to be presented. A one to three hour course would simply provide a mere familiarization with general stress management. A one day course allows some practice time to try out some of the general stress management skills which are taught. A two day course provides considerably more information and opportunities to practice the stress skills.

The general stress management course can be named in any way the instructor deems necessary. The course is designed to familiarize people with the nature and effects of general stress in every day life. The relationship between home stress and work stress is shown. It is pointed out that stress can be a very positive, as well as a negative force. The course provides many helpful stress management techniques which can be learned quickly and which have benefited many people during the last two decades.

C. Length: Between one hour and two days

D. Format: For one to three hour courses- lecture, illustrated lecture. For one and two day course - lecture, illustrated lecture, demonstration and discussion

E. Technical assistance: Shorter version of the course are taught by

STRESS MANAGEMENT

emergency services instructors or mental health professionals. The one and two day course are usually taught by mental health professionals. In any case the course should be reviewed by a mental health professional who is very familiar with the topic of general stress management.

F. Course objectives:

For one to three hour courses:

At the conclusion of this program the learner will be able to:

1. Identify the various types of stress.

2. Define general stress and identify positive and negative aspects of stress

3. Describe the General Adaptation Syndrome as a normal reaction to a sudden, unusual demand on the mind or body.

4. List general stress management techniques which help to mitigate stress and, maintain health

For one and two day courses:
   (The objectives listed above may apply along with those listed below)
   At the conclusion of this course the learner will be able to:

5. Demonstrate by practice an understanding of stress management techniques such as deep breathing, progressive muscle relaxation, and guided imagery.

6. Construct a personal plan of stress management.

G. Title: Overview of general stress management

H. Domain of learning: cognitive for short programs. Cognitive, affective and psychomotor for one and two day programs

I. Levels of instruction: short programs - preparation /presentation One and two day - preparation, presentation, application, and evaluation

J. References for both short and long programs:

- Mitchell, J.T. and Bray, G.P. (1990) Emergency Services Stress. Englewood Cliffs, NJ: Brady Communications, Prentice Hall.

- Everly, G.S. (1989). A Clinical Guide to the Treatment of the Human Stress Response. NY: Plenum Press.

- Girdano, D.A., Everly, G.S. and Dusek, D.E. (1993) Controlling Stress and Tension: A holistic Approach, 4 edition. Englewood Cliffs, NJ: Prentice Hall

- Federal Emergency Management Agency (FEMA) (1991) Stress Management: Model program for Firefighter Well Being. Washington, DC: US Fire Administration.

K. Audio visual support: Slide projectors, overhead projectors, video tapes, audio tapes, etc. at the discretion of the instructor.

II. Course Outlines

A. One hour program outline:

(expand for two hour program)

- Introduction
- Define stress
- Eustress
- Distress
- General Adaptation Syndrome
- Elements of healthy living
- General suggestions on managing stress
    - flexibility
    - humor
    - time management

- time outs

- relaxation

- balance in life.

- exercise

- rest

- family life

- friends

B. Three hours Program Outline:

- Introduction
- Define stress
- Relate General Stress to other types of stress
- Causes of Stress
- Effects of stress
- Eustress
- Distress
- Stress and productivity
- Best level of stress
- General Adaptation Syndrome
- Survival skills for stress management
- Mental outlook affecting stress
- Specific techniques to mitigate stress

  - diet

  - rest

  - exercise

  - flexibility

STRESS MANAGEMENT

- humor

- time management

- changing environment

- balance in life

- vacations

- family life

- friends

- relaxation

C. One day Program Outline

One day general stress management programs are easier to teach since they allow considerably more time to cover the topics and also allow some time for practicing the stress management techniques.

The topical outline is as follows:

1. Morning Session:

- Introduction
- Define stress
- Clarify the relationship of general stress to other types of stress
- Eustress
- Stress and productivity
- Distress
- General Adaptation Syndrome
- Causes of stress
- Effects of stress

    - cognitive

        - physical

        - emotional

        - behavioral

- Cumulative stress

- Causes of cumulative stress

- Effects of cumulative stress on performance

- Effects of cumulative stress on life

- Best level of stress

2. Afternoon Session:

- Surviving the stress onslaught

- Attitude

- Balance

- Care for oneself

- Care for another

- Techniques of survival

        - diet

        - exercise

        - humor

        - flexibility

        - time management

        - altering environment

        - rest

        - relaxation

        - balance in life

        - family life

STRESS MANAGEMENT

- friends

- vacations

- Practice (guided) time for skills

    deep breathing

    Progressive muscle relaxation

    Guided imagery

- Question and answer

- Course conclusion

D. Two Day Program Outline

There are many benefits to teaching general stress by means of a two day program. One of the most important is that the practice sessions for the various skills can start early in the course and continue through the program. The learning potential is greater with repetition of some of the skills which is necessary in the two day program.

1. Morning day one:

- Introduction to stress management

- Get students to stand, stretch, turn toward the people on each side of them and introduce themselves

- Define stress

- Relate general stress to other types of stress

- Eustress

- Stress and productivity

- Causes of stress

- Distress

- Practice deep breathing

    - very deep breathing

- deep breathing
- normal breathing
- General Adaptation Syndrome
- The pluses and minuses of the General Adaptation Syndrome
- Effects of stress
  - cognitive
  - physical
  - emotional
  - behavioral

2. Afternoon of day one
- Practice session on progressive muscle relaxation
- Cumulative stress
- Phases of cumulative stress
  - warning
  - mild symptoms
  - entrenched
  - severe
- Signs and symptoms of cumulative stress
- practice session on deep breathing and progressive muscle relaxation combined
- Individual and organizational effects of stress
- Effects on the family
- Question and answer period

3. Morning of day two:
- Remaining questions and clarifications from the previous

day

- Guided imagery practice session
- General stress management strategy
- Various types of stress management techniques

  - changing stress

  - changing self

  - cushioning techniques

- practice session combining deep breathing and guided imagery

4. Afternoon of day two:

- Specific stress management techniques
- Time management
- Environmental engineering
- Diet
- Exercise
- Healthy living
- Family life
- Recreation
- Rest
- Relaxation
- Final practice session combining deep breathing, progressive muscle relaxation and guided imagery to music
- Group discussion
- Question and answers
- Course conclusion

STRESS MANAGEMENT

CRITICAL INCIDENT STRESS COURSE OUTLINE

The next four courses to be described below are critical incident stress (CIS) familiarization programs. They are not a CISD course. These courses in no way substitute for a CISD course. The CISD course description stands alone in the next chapter.

I. CIS Course Overview

A. Idea: Critical incident stress (CIS) is an important topic which is being taught to emergency personnel in many parts of the world. It is being taught by mental health professionals and peer support personnel alike. CISM teams are organizing this type of training on a regular basis. There is a need for an overview course which will describe critical incident stress and which will familiarize operations people with CIS and the interventions which exist to counteract it.

B. Description: The CIS familiarization course has been designed to be taught in a flexible manner which will assist emergency teams who have only a limited time available for training. These courses are short, contain easy to learn concepts and can provide enough information in a short period of time so that the learner will understand CIS and its impact and be ready to call for assistance from a trained critical incident stress team.

C. Length: The CIS familiarization course can range from between one hour to two full days. Course length depends on the needs of the organization and the personnel in it as well as the amount of resources available to support the training.

D. Format: The familiarization course for CIS is a classroom presentation which uses lecture or illustrated lecture in its shorter versions and lecture, illustrated lecture demonstration and discussion in the two day versions.

E. Technical Assistance required: The course should be reviewed by a mental health professional. Frequently it is team taught by mental health professionals and peer support personnel. Mental health professionals are often asked to guest lecture in such courses.

F. Course Objectives: The shorter versions of this course may use the following objectives:

At the conclusion of this course, the learner will be able to:

1. Define Critical Incident Stress and contrast it to general stress.

2. Cite the causes of CIS.

3. List the cognitive, physical, emotional and behavioral manifestation of CIS.

4. Define Critical Incident Stress Debriefing (CISD).

5. Describe the general make-up and functions of a CISD team and know how to call for one if it is needed

The one and two day versions of the CIS course may have additional course objectives written including the following:

At the conclusion of this course, the learner will be able to:

6. Describe on scene support services and discuss how they are employed

7. Define defusings and discuss when they are used.

8. Distinguish between defusing and debriefings

9. Define the term, Critical Incident Stress Management (CISM)

10. Discuss other CISM team services such as significant other support, disaster services, follow up and education

11. Discuss the importance of education in the management of CIS.

G. Domains of learning: Cognitive and affective in the shorter courses and cognitive, affective and psychomotor in the long courses.

H. Levels of instruction: Preparation and presentation in the shorter programs and preparation, presentation, application and evaluation in the longer courses.

I. References: The following texts will be useful in assisting instructors to present CIS material:

- Federal Emergency Management Agency (FEMA). (1991). <u>Stress Management: Model Program for Maintaining Firefighter Well Being</u>. Washington, DC: FEMA, US Fire Administration

- Mitchell, J.T. and Bray, G.P. (1990). <u>Emergency Services Stress.</u> Englewood Cliffs, NJ: Brady Communications, Prentice Hall.

- Mitchell, J.T. and Everly, G.S. (1993). <u>Critical Incident Stress Debriefing (CISD): An operations manual for the prevention of traumatic stress among emergency services and disaster workers</u>. Ellicott City, MD: Chevron Publishing Corporation.

- Reese, J.T. and Horn, J.M. (1991). <u>Critical Incidents in Policing, Revised</u>. Washington, DC: US Government Printing Office.

- van der Kolk, B.A. (1987). <u>Psychological Trauma</u>. Washington, DC: American Psychiatric Press, Inc.

J. Audio visual support: slide projector, video player and monitor, audio cassette, flip charts, blackboard at the discretion of the instructor.

II Course Outlines

A. One to Two Hour Program Outline:

- Introduction

- Define general stress

- Definition of Critical incident Stress

- Contrast general stress with CIS

- Cause of CIS

- Effects of CIS

> a. cognitive
>
> b. physical
>
> c. emotional
>
> d. behavioral

- General survival tactics for CIS

- CISD

- Calling for help

B. Three Hour Program Outline

The outline of the three hour program does not differ substantially from that of the one to two hour program. The small amount of additional time enables the instructor to cover some of the information in more detail. An example of that expansion in depth is shown in the outline below.

- Introduction

- Nature of stress

- Critical Incident Stress

- Contrast general stress with CIS

    - general stress is universal and typically, at low levels, a positive form of stress. Necessary for health.

    - critical incident stress is directly related to the occurrence of a traumatic event. It can deteriorate, performance, health and personal life. Occasionally needs outside support

- Causes of CIS - major traumatic situations

- death of emergency worker

- serious line of duty injury

- disaster

- police shooting

- emergency worker's suicide

- baby / child death

- killing / injuring civilian

- prolonged incident with loss

- severe threat to emergency personnel

- any significant event

- Effects of stress

    - cognitive symptoms

    - physical symptoms

    - emotional symptoms

    - behavioral symptoms

- General CIS survival tactics

    - resting crews

    - feeding crews

    - fluid replacement

    - limiting exposure

    - cutting stimulus bombardment during rest breaks

    - changing assignments

    - post-event defusing

    - debriefing if necessary

- CISD overview

- The CISM team and calling for help

C. One Day Program Outline

1. Morning

- Introduction
- Nature of stress
- Types of stress
    - General (Eustress vs. Distress)
    - Cumulative
    - Critical Incident Stress
    - Post Traumatic Stress Disorder
- Contrast general and CIS
    - all people have general stress. Necessary for life. Usually positive. Becomes negative if it is perceived as negative or if excessive.
    - CIS is result of traumatic event. Normal reaction to abnormal event. Sets stage for Post Traumatic Stress Disorder if not resolved. Sometimes needs intervention to reduce chances of Post Traumatic Stress Disorder
- Causes of CIS
    - line of duty death
    - line of duty injury
    - police shooting
    - disaster
    - emergency worker suicide
    - baby / child death

CRITICAL INCIDENT STRESS

- extreme threat to emergency worker

- prolonged incident which ends in loss

- victims known to operations personnel

- death / injury of civilian caused by operations

- any other significant event

- Effects of CIS

    - cognitive

    - physical

    - emotional

    - behavioral

2. Afternoon

- Surviving Critical Incident Stress

    A. Prevention tactics

        - pre incident education

        - command / supervisor training

        - rotation of crews

        - rest times

        - limit exposure

        - team work

        - leadership

        - administration support

        - written stress policies

        - written stress procedures

        - etc.

    B. Management tactics

- peer support

- defusings

- debriefings

- significant other support

- etc.

- CISD

- what it is?

- what it is not?

- who needs it?

- who provides it?

- how do units call for it?

- how does it work?

- what is a CISD or CISM team?

- Question and answers

- Course conclusion

D. Two Day Program

It would be extremely rare for a CISM team to provide a full two day Critical Incident Stress course which was not a debriefing training. It is difficult to imagine an emergency services unit which would need a full two days unless they were going to set up or participate in an organized CISD program. A full two day course is generally not a recommended program.

In the rare situation, however, in which a two day course was required, some additional information might be added into the one day program which was outlined above. Here is a list of the possible topics which could be added into the course to make it a full two days:

- Post Traumatic Stress Disorder, an overview

- A more detailed list of CIS symptoms

- The video "CISD: Techniques of Debriefing"
- A defusing demonstration
- A detailed description of a debriefing
- A student involved discussion.
- A case review
- A discussion of a comprehensive program of Critical Incident Stress Management

    - chaplain program

    - significant other support

    - etc.

- A guest speaker or a panel presenting their own stories
- Contrast cumulative stress and critical incident stress
- Etc.

COMMAND OFFICERS STRESS SURVIVAL GUIDE

I. Course Overview

Command officers and supervisors have some of the most difficult tasks in the emergency services business. They must maintain control over the operation and the activities of their personnel, draw the event to a successful conclusion, keep the situation contained and simultaneously assure the safety and well being of their personnel. All too often they are thrown into leadership positions without specific training in critical incident stress management. They may not know what signs and symptoms of distress to look for in their personnel and therefore may not call for the services of a CISM/CISD team when it is necessary. CIS training is a necessity for supervisory personnel.

A. Idea: A course to provide supervisors and commanders with the basic knowledge to prevent critical incident stress and to identify and begin the intervention process for distressed personnel under their supervision.

B. Description: This course prepares supervisors and command officers to recognize and deal with critical incident stress in their personnel before it can disrupt the operations of the group or the individuals who serve in those groups. Personnel involved in this class learn some basic indicators of critical incident stress which distinguish it from disciplinary problems or personality disorders.

C. Length: Either three hours or one full day.

D. Format: The course utilizes lecture, illustrated lecture and provides handout material to cover the material.

E. Technical Assistance: The course may be taught by well trained CISM peers or mental health professionals. An ideal combination is a teaching team made up of a peer and a mental health professional.

F. Course objectives: At the conclusion of this course the participant will be able to:

1. Define the terms, crisis, stress, critical incident stress, cumulative stress, and Post Traumatic Stress Disorder.

2. Describe the relationship between routine or general stress and cumulative stress.

COMMAND OFFICERS COURSE

3. Describe the relationship between critical incident stress and Post Traumatic Stress Disorder.

4. Identify some of the basic indicators that an emergency worker's behavior is stress related as opposed to a disciplinary problem or a personality problem.

5. List the techniques to prevent critical incident stress in their personnel.

6. List the techniques to reduce stress during on scene operations.

7. Identify the sources of support available (including the CISM team) when after-action support is necessary for one's personnel.

8. Describe the general functions of a CISM team.

9. Define a defusing and a CISD.

10. State the importance of follow up services for one's personnel after encountering traumatic stress.

G. Title: Command Officers Stress Survival Course

H. Lesson Number: Instructors should break this course into smaller lesson components. The subdivision of the course is at the instructor's discretion.

I. Domains of learning: Cognitive and affective.

J. Levels of instruction: Preparation, presentation, application and evaluation depending on the lesson being covered.

K. References: Mitchell and Bray (1990); Mitchell and Everly (1993).

L. Audiovisual support: Slide projector or overhead projector, screen, video tape player and monitor, audio cassette player, other at the discretion of the instructor.

II. Course Outlines:

A. Three Hours

It is difficult to provide useful information to supervisory or command
staff with less than a three hour time block. There is simply too
much material to present in less time.

COURSE OUTLINE   ESSENTIAL TEACHING POINTS

• Introduction

• Types of stress

   - general   * all have it

               * general stress can be + or -

               * it is not bad unless it becomes
                 excessive or prolonged

               * it can lead to cumulative stress

   - cumulative   * a chronic state of disturbing
                 stress which can cause physical and
                 emotional illness and changes in
                 personality over time

   - critical incident   * also called "traumatic stress"

     stress   * not caused by general stress or
                 cumulative stress but produced
                 by a specific terrible event.

               * all people are vulnerable

COMMAND OFFICERS COURSE

* some may react more strongly than others

* usually resolves in a reasonable period of time

* may need a debriefing or some other brief support services

* can turn into a serious problem for a few people if it is not resolved

* good supervisors should be able to recognize the problem

* good supervisors should call for appropriate help from a CISM team when it is necessary

* good supervisors should know the signals that CISM help is necessary

-Post traumatic Stress Disorder

* small percentage of emergency personnel develop PTSD if critical incident stress is not properly resolved

* good supervisors can recognize the early signs that critical incident stress is not being resolved

* supervisors should refer individuals for professional assistance if symptoms of critical incident stress do not resolve in a reasonable time frame

* signs of unresolved critical
  incident stress include:

  - continued stress symptoms
    in personnel despite time
    passage or the fact that
    help has already been
    given

  - intensifying stress
    symptoms despite time
    passage or help given

  - intrusive images (dreams
    or flashbacks)

  - emotional numbing

  - fear of repetition of the
    event

  - hyper startle response

  - loss of interest in usually
    enjoyable tasks

  - depression

  - intensified anxiety

  - emotional outbursts

  - withdrawal from others

  - memory dysfunction

  - other significant signs

• Recognizing   * Cognitive symptoms
  critical   * Physical symptoms
  incident stress   * Emotional symptoms

COMMAND OFFICERS COURSE

* Behavioral symptoms

- Preventing critical
  incident stress

  * Pre incident education
  * Planning
  * Drills / practice
  * Pre deployment briefings

- Mitigating Operational
  Stress

  * Frequent information /feedback to staff
  * Frequent rest breaks
  * Cold or hot environments might require more frequent rest breaks
  * Rest areas away from stimuli
  * 12 hour limit for same scene
  * Assure proper rehabilitation sector
  * Provide hand washing facilities
  * Provide medical support to staff
  * Monitor hyper- or hypo- thermia
  * Proper food
  * Limit fat sugar and salt
  * Fluid replacement
  * Provide drinking water
  * Provide fruit juices
  * Limit use of caffeine products
  * CISM on scene support services

* Monitor signs of emotional distress

* Cut overall stimuli at incident

* Give clear orders to personnel

* Avoid conflicting orders to staff

* Delegate authority to sector officers

* Frequent rest breaks for officers

* Credit people for proper actions

* Limit criticism to absolute minimum

* Utilize a staging area for uninvolved personnel

* Limit exposure to disturbing sites and sounds

* Announce time periodically

* Rotate crews to alternate duties

• After Action Support
* Thank personnel for their work

* Provide demobilization services on large scale incident

* Utilize services of CISM team

* Arrange defusing for unusual events

* Consider debriefing for personnel if it appears necessary

* Consult with CISM team

* Allow follow up services by CISM

team members
* Critique incident

* Teach new procedures from
lessons learned

B. One Day

A full one day Command Officers Stress Survival Course is the ideal program. All the material presented in the three hour program above can be presented as well as additional material presented in the course outline which follows.

COURSE OUTLINE   ESSENTIAL TEACHING POINTS

• Introduction
• Course overview
• Definition of stress

* state of physical and psychological
arousal common to all biological
organisms

• Types of stress
- general   * all have it

* general stress can be positive or
negative

* it is not bad unless it
becomes excessive or prolonged

* it can lead to cumulative stress

- cumulative   * a chronic state of disturbing

stress which can cause physical and emotional illness and changes in personality over time

* takes months or years to develop

* may be a combination of work and home life

* often referred to as "burnout"

* often needs professional help for recovery especially if in late stages

* develops in four stages

      - early warning

      - mild symptoms

      - entrenched

      - severe symptoms

* characterized by gradually declining performance, increasing problems on job

* early symptoms

      - vague anxiety

      - boredom

      - general fatigue

      - boredom

* mild symptoms

      - all early plus

      - irritability

      - chronic tension

      - depression

Page 115

- frustration
- frequent sighs
- sleep disturbance
- chronic worry
- lost of interest in work
- more frequent colds
- mild rashes
- headaches
- withdrawal from others
- etc.

* entrenched symptoms
    - chronic depression
    - loss of joy of life
    - chronic anger
    - increased drinking
    - thoughts of suicide
    - emotional outbursts
    - marital or relationship discord
    - conflict with fellow workers
    - conflict with supervisors
    - increasing discipline problems
    - increased self destructive behaviors like smoking
    - withdrawal from loved ones

- loss of trust in others

- increasing paranoia

- loss of ambition

- tendency to blame others

- inability to take responsibility for one's own actions

- minor property destruction

- acting out behaviors

* severe symptoms

- rage reactions

- homicidal thinking

- suicidal thinking / acts

- easily angered

- verbally violent outbursts

- acts of violence

- threats to others

- excessive drinking

- severe depression

- severe paranoia

- break up of relationships over minor issues

- compulsive thinking about bothersome topics

- easily frustrated

- sense of hopelessness

COMMAND OFFICERS COURSE

- sense of helplessness

- seriously declining
  performance

- most symptoms from
  previous levels

- etc.

• Management of
  cumulative stress
  reactions

* stress management education

* balance in life - work, home, etc.

* recreation

* vacations

* limiting overtime

* emphasis on home life

* professional counseling when
  needed

* exercise

* proper food

* clear job expectations

* reduction of one worker
  performing two conflicting jobs

* effective leadership

* administrative support

* stress reduction techniques

* healthy living

* effective training

* etc.

Page 118

- critical incident
  stress

* also called "traumatic stress"

* not caused by general stress or cumulative stress but produced by a specific terrible event.

* all people are vulnerable

* emergency personnel may be more vulnerable because of exposure to traumatic events

* some may react more strongly than others

* usually resolves in a reasonable period of time

* may need a debriefing or some other brief support services

* can turn into a serious problem for a few people if it is not resolved

* good supervisors should be able to recognize the problem

* good supervisors should call for appropriate help from a CISM team when it is necessary

* good supervisors should know the signals that CISM help is necessary

-Post Traumatic
Stress Disorder

* small percentage of emergency personnel develop PTSD if

COMMAND OFFICERS COURSE

critical incident stress is not properly resolved (estimated between 4 - 16%)

* good supervisors can recognize the early signs that critical incident stress is not being resolved

* supervisors should refer individuals for professional assistance if symptoms of critical incident stress do not resolve in a reasonable time frame

* signs of unresolved critical incident stress include:

  - continued stress symptoms in personnel despite time passage or the fact that help has already been given

  - intensifying stress symptoms despite time passage or help

  - intrusive images (dreams or flashbacks)

  - emotional numbing

  - fear of repetition of the event

  - hyper startle response

  - loss of interest in usually enjoyable tasks

- depression
- intensified anxiety
- emotional outbursts
- withdrawal from others
- memory dysfunction
- other significant signs

- Recognizing critical incident stress
  * Cognitive symptoms
  * Physical symptoms
  * Emotional symptoms
  * Behavioral symptoms

- Preventing critical incident stress
  * Pre incident education
  * Planning
  * Drills / practice
  * Pre deployment briefings

- Mitigating operational stress
  * Frequent information /feedback to staff
  * Frequent rest breaks
  * Cold or hot environments might require more frequent rest breaks
  * Rest areas away from stimuli
  * 12 hour limit for same scene
  * Assure proper rehabilitation sector

COMMAND OFFICERS COURSE

* Provide lavatory facilities

* Provide hand washing facilities

* Provide medical support to staff

* Monitor hyper- or hypo-thermia

* Proper food

* Limit fat, sugar and salt

* Fluid replacement

* Provide drinking water

* Provide fruit juices

* Limit use of caffeine products

* CISM on scene support services

* Monitor signs of emotional distress

* Cut overall stimuli at incident

* Give clear orders to personnel

* Avoid conflicting orders to staff

* Delegate authority to sector officers

* Frequent rest breaks for officers

* Back up officers

* Sectorization of the incident

* Delegation of authority

* Credit people for proper actions

* Limit criticism to absolute minimum

* Utilize a staging area for
  uninvolved personnel

* Limit exposure to disturbing sites

and sounds

* Announce time periodically

* Rotate crews to alternate duties

* etc.

- After Action   * Thank personnel for their work
  Support

  * Provide demobilization services on large scale incident

  * Utilize services of CISM team

  * Arrange defusing for unusual events

  * Consider debriefing for personnel if it appears necessary

  * Consult with CISM team

  * Allow follow up services by CISM team members

  * Critique incident

  * Teach new procedures from lessons learned

- Some indicators   * identifiable traumatic event
  of critical   indicates CIS
  incident stress   * reactions begin with event in CIS
  vs. disciplinary   * reactions worsen after event
  problems or   in CIS
  character disorders * CIS symptoms follow expected

patterns

* sudden changes are common in CIS

* CIS symptoms usually reduce with help and with the passage of time

* disciplinary problems have a long and diffuse history

* problems may have preexisted entry into the job

* identifiable traumatic event(s) missing

* problems may exist in several important areas of the person's life

* problems do not easily resolve over time even with help

- Critical Incident Stress Management Resources

  * CISM team
  * Employee assistance programs
  * Chaplain services
  * Psychologists
  * Peer counselors
  * Respected officers

- General Functions

  * Pre incident education
  * On scene support services

Of CISM Teams
* Defusings
* Demobilizations
* Debriefings
* Individual consultations
* Significant other support
* Follow up services
* Specialty debriefings
* informal discussions

• Defusing
* short group process
* provided by CISM trained personnel
* frequently provided by peer support personnel
* may be provided by a combined team of peers and mental health professionals
* given within 8-12 hours
* provided after incident is complete
* usually lasts under one hour
* has three parts
     - introduction
     - exploration
     - information
* personnel do not have to speak
* not an incident critique
* must be kept confidential

COMMAND OFFICERS COURSE

* may eliminate need for full debriefing

* may enhance debriefing if it still necessary

• Critical Incident Stress Debriefing

* group process

* usually provided 24-72 hours after incident

* may be earlier or later depending on group's readiness

* structured discussion of a traumatic event

* provided by a team of CISM trained personnel

* team includes mental health professional and several peer support personnel

* not a critique

* not psychotherapy

* lasts 2-3 hours

* has seven phases

- introduction

- fact

- thought

- reaction

- symptoms

- teaching

                                    - re-entry

                        * followed up by one-on-one support

• Follow up services   * extremely important

                            * assures success of intervention

                            * individual contacts

                            * telephone contacts

                            * small group meetings

                            * chaplain visits

                            * home visits

                            * station visits

                            * ride-a-long programs

                            * significant other support

                            * family support services

                            * etc.

Summary

This chapter provides overviews of fifteen crisis intervention and stress management courses. It includes several sample outlines for one and two day crisis intervention courses as well as stress management and critical incident stress management programs. The courses are designed as either stand alone courses or as samples of course outlines which can be easily adapted by a wide range of organizations. Instructors should find these outlines invaluable when they are preparing courses for emergency personnel and disaster workers.

The next chapter presents a detailed course outline and teaching guide for the basic Critical Incident Stress Debriefing Training course. It will be extremely helpful to instructors who qualify to teach the basic CISD course.

CHAPTER 6

The Basic Critical Incident Stress Debriefing (CISD) Course

GENERAL TOPICAL OUTLINE FOR A TWO DAY PROGRAM

The following topics will be covered during the basic CISD course. The topical outline below represents the content to be presented during a two day basic course. More information may be added to a basic course, but, the addition of expanded material will necessitate a lengthening of the course beyond the two day minimum.

Day 1

Course Introduction

Nature of Stress

Types of Stress

    a. General

    b. Cumulative

    c. Critical Incident Stress

    d. Post Traumatic Stress Disorder

Emergency Services Stress

Types of Critical Incidents

Personality of Emergency Services Personnel

Rudiments of team organization and management
    - (optional session refer to CISD manual)

Ten basic interventions of CISM

On scene support services

Defusings

Demobilizations

Question and answers

Debriefing video

Day 2

Debriefing overview

Debriefing details

Debriefing demonstration

Question and answers

Course conclusion

STANDARD CISD LESSON PLANS

Day one: Topics one through twelve

Topic 1:   INTRODUCTION TO THE BASIC CISD COURSE

<u>Time</u>: 15 minutes

<u>Level of Instruction</u>: Preparation - motivating the learner and setting up the atmosphere necessary to understand both Critical Incident Stress and the Critical Incident Stress Debriefing (CISD) process.

<u>Objectives</u>:

1) At the conclusion of this topic the instructor or a person designated

to do so will have provided the students with a brief introduction and or a biographical sketch of the instructor or the instructors.

2) At the conclusion of this topic the instructor or a designated person should have made any necessary announcements regarding the course or the facilities in which it is being held.

3) At the conclusion of this topic the instructor or course coordinator will have provided sufficient information pertaining to the following topics:

> * proper registration for the course and completion of registration forms
>
> * the goals and objectives of the course
>
> * The mechanisms for the course management including:
>
> * question and answer periods and the best times to ask questions
>
> * demonstrations of course concepts
>
> * basic rules and procedures of the course
>
> * breaks
>
> * certificates
>
> * instructor contact phone numbers and address
>
> * cautions about the intense nature of some course content, etc.

4) At the conclusion of this topic the instructor will have obtained basic information regarding the professions of the students. That is, the instructor should have a reasonable knowledge of the make up of the audience by professional groups.

5) At the conclusion of this topic the students will have been able to clarify their expectations and instructor information by means of a brief question and answer period.

Materials:

Registration forms

Textbook: (optional) Mitchell and Everly, 1993; workbook

Student workbook and / or handout packet :

appropriate CISD articles

study materials

miscellaneous handouts

information on local teams

information on ICISF's international network of CISM teams

other pertinent information

(students typically provide their own note pads and writing materials)

Recommended Equipment: Blackboard or flip chart

1/2 inch video player and television monitor

cassette tape player

slide projector

screen

overhead projector

microphone

podium

table

ice water for instructor(s)

other equipment according to instructor need

(Note: The above equipment is only suggested. Each instructor has different needs and the equipment required to teach the course should be provided

according to the instructor requirements.)

Audio Visual Aids:

Instructors should develop a collection of slides, video tapes, audio tapes, overheads and other audio visual aids to enhance the learning experience during the course. Little, if any, audio visual support is necessary while presenting the introduction. The need for audio visual support increases as later topics are presented. It is, of course, the obligation of the instructor to arrive early and assure that all audio-visual equipment is properly functioning and that the audio visual aids are in a state of readiness.

References:

There are numerous articles in the literature which describe the Critical Incident Stress problem and the Critical Incident Stress Debriefing process. Instructors should be familiar with these publications. In addition, instructors should be familiar with:

Mitchell, J.T. and Bray, G.P. (1990). Emergency Services Stress: Guidelines for Preserving the Health and Careers of Emergency Services Personnel. Englewood Cliffs, NJ: Brady Company, Prentice Hall Publishers.

Mitchell, J.T. and Everly, G.S. (1993). Critical Incident Stress Debriefing (CISD): An Operations Manual for the Prevention of Traumatic Stress among Emergency Services and Disaster Workers. Ellicott City, MD: Chevron Publishing.

Note: One of the most important elements of the introduction is a clear statement which warns the students that some of the material covered in the Critical Incident Stress Debriefing course is emotionally intense and may inadvertently stir up some uncomfortable feelings which are associated with the student's past painful experiences. Students should be advised that it is normal for the course material to stir up these old feelings, but, the student should seek professional help if the feelings become excessive or if they do not become resolved in a reasonable period of time (several days).

TOPIC 2: NATURE OF STRESS, TYPES OF STRESS AND ELEMENTS OF EMERGENCY SERVICES STRESS

<u>Time</u>: 20 minutes

<u>Level of Instruction</u>: Preparation of the student and presentation of concepts.

<u>Objectives</u>: Upon completing this topic the student should be able to:

* Obtain, by means of lecture and a handout, information regarding the nature of general stress.

* Obtain, by means of lecture and a handout, information regarding cumulative stress.

* Obtain, by means of the workbook or a handout, a list of signs and symptoms of cumulative stress.

* Explain the term "Cumulative Stress".

* Explain the terms "Critical Incident Stress" and "Traumatic Stress".

* Obtain, by means of a handout, a list of cognitive, physical, emotional and behavioral symptoms of stress.

* Discuss emergency services stress and explain how it differs from general stress.

* Obtain, by means of a handout, information regarding the signs and symptoms of critical incident stress.

* Describe the causes of critical incident stress.

* Explain the difference between immediate and delayed critical incident stress.

* Discuss the impact of delayed stress on the emergency worker.

Materials:

>Workbook and / or handouts on:

>>General stress

>>Cumulative stress

>>General stress symptom lists

>>Cumulative stress symptoms lists

>>Signs and symptoms of CIS

>Textbooks (see recommendations under topic 1 above)

Equipment: Audio visual equipment as suggested under equipment in topic 1 above. Equipment utilization is according to instructor requirements.

Audio Visual Aids: It is recommended that instructors utilize slides or overhead transparencies to highlight important points in this section.

References: Same as Topic 1.

PRESENTATION: (Topic 2) Emergency Services Stress

TEACHING POINTS	MAIN FACTS TO BE PRESENTED
I. Topic overview	A. Stress is normal
	1. all people have it
	2. not usually harmful
	3. Can be positive
	4. often enhances productivity (Eustress)

5. excessive stress is dysfunctional and pathogenic (Distress)

6. prolonged stress can be harmful

B. Cumulative stress

1. builds up over time

2. often called "burnout"

3. mixes home and work stress

4. deterioration of person over time

5. erodes personal resources

C. Traumatic Stress

1. also called "Critical Incident Stress"

2. cognitive, physical, emotional and behavioral

D. Emergency Services Stress

1. adds general stress with specific stress associated with emergency work

2. subcategory of Traumatic Stress

II. Causes of CIS   Background information

                           1. history of CIS

                           2. types of events

                           3. critical incidents:

-line of duty deaths

-line of duty serious injuries

-suicide of emergency person

-disaster or multicasualty incident

-police shooting

-accidental killing or wounding of civilian

-significant events involving children

-prolonged incidents ending in failure

-known victims

-any significant event which overwhelms rescuers

III. Effects of CIS   A. Cognitive symptoms

B. Physical symptoms

C. Emotional symptoms

D. Behavioral symptoms

IV. Immediate vs. Delayed   A. Immediate CIS (usually shows up in first 24 hours)

B. Delayed CIS (after first 24 hours)

TOPIC 3: TYPES OF CRITICAL INCIDENTS

Time: 15 minutes

Level of Instruction: Prepare the student, present the new concepts. Request involvement from the learner by asking them to suggest situations which could be considered "critical incidents".

Objectives: When instruction in this topic is concluded, the student should be able to:

* List the most common critical incidents.

* Describe the impact that children have on emergency personnel.

* Discuss a broad spectrum of incidents which are likely to distress emergency personnel.

* Discuss the impact of line of duty death on the emergency services.

* Explain the effect of a multi-casualty incident on the personnel.

* Explain the difference between an automatic debriefing and a mandatory debriefing.

Materials:

Workbook and handouts on critical incidents

Equipment: Audio visual equipment as suggested under equipment in topic 1 above. Equipment should meet instructor requirements.

Audio Visual Aids: Slides or overhead transparencies are recommended to highlight important features as this topic is presented.

References: It is recommended that the students be referred to the numerous articles which have been written on CIS as well as the texts recommended in topic 1 above.

PRESENTATION: TYPES OF CRITICAL INCIDENTS

An "automatic" CISD is one which is provided whenever one of the first five of the "terrible ten" incidents occur. "Automatic" CISD's are written into the policies and procedures manuals of emergency organizations.

TEACHING POINTS	MAIN FACTS TO BE PRESENTED
I. "Terrible Ten"	A. Automatic CISD Triggers
	1. Line of Duty Death
	2. Serious line of duty injury
	3. Emergency worker suicide
	4. Multi-Casualty Incident
	5. Police shooting or injury or death to a civilian as a result of operational procedures
	B. Potential CISD Triggers
	6. Significant events involving children
	7. Victim relative or known to helper
	8. Failed mission after extensive effort
	9. Excessive media interest
	10. Any powerful event
II. Miscellaneous Triggers	A. Repetitive horrible events

B. Symbolic events

C. Multiple events

D. Events with personal meaning

E. Threatening events

F. Administrative abandonment

G. Other

III. Mandatory debriefing

A "mandatory" CISD is one that is ordered by supervisors or commanders. It may be one of the automatic debriefings listed above or it may be outside of the usual list. The key point is that supervisors or commanders think it is important enough to order people to attend the CISD.

TOPIC 4: PERSONALITY PROFILE OF EMERGENCY SERVICES PERSONNEL

Time: 15 minutes

Level of Instruction: one, two and three - Prepare the learner, present the concepts, and assist the learners in making applications. Involve the learner in the learning process by inviting questions and comments related to the topic.

Objectives: At the conclusion of this topic the student will be able to:

* Describe the personality profile of emergency services workers.

* List the most prominent features of the emergency personality.

Materials:

Workbook and / or handouts on the personality profile of emergency

personnel

Texts as previously suggested in topic 1 above

Equipment: Audio visual equipment as required by the instructor.

Audio Visual Aids: Slides or overhead transparencies are recommended for this topic.

References: See recommendations in topic 1 above.

PRESENTATION: PROTOTYPIC PERSONALITY PROFILE OF EMERGENCY PERSONNEL

TEACHING POINTS	MAIN FACTS TO BE PRESENTED
I. Prototypic Emergency personality	A. Similar between services
	B. Similar within service
	C. Necessary for job
	D. Normal personality traits not pathology
II. Key factors	A. Control needs
	B. Obsessive traits
	C. Compulsive traits
	D. Action oriented
	E. High need for stimulation
	F. Need for immediate gratification
	G. Difficulty saying no
	H. Rescue personality
	I. Family oriented
	J. Highly dedicated

K. Internally motivated

L. High tolerance for stress

TOPIC 5: RUDIMENTS OF TEAM ORGANIZATION AND MANAGEMENT (OPTIONAL TOPIC)

Many instructors prefer to hold a separate session on this topic outside of the course. The appendices in Mitchell and Everly, 1993 are most helpful in presenting this topic.

<u>Time</u>: 30 minutes

<u>Level of Instruction</u>: one, two and three - Prepare the learner, present the concepts and assist the learners in making applications of the material. Encourage discussion and questions from the participants.

<u>Objectives</u>: Upon completion of this topic the student should be able to:

* Describe the steps necessary to establish a CISM team

* Explain the minimal requirements to keep a team functional

* Discuss the basic management principles associated with a CISM team

* List the three main strategies for team maintenance

* Define the main leadership roles on a CISM team

* Discuss the steering committee concept related to CISM

* Discuss the basic principles for choosing team membership

<u>Materials</u>:

Workbook or handouts on team organization

Recommended texts (see topic 1)

Equipment: Audio visual equipment as suggested in topic 1.

Audio Visual Aids: Slides or overhead transparencies are recommended for this topic.

References:

Kennedy-Ewing, L. (1988). Operational and Training Guide for the Critical Incident Stress Management Program of Delaware County, Pennsylvania. Media, PA: Department of Human Resources, 600 N. Jackson St. Media, PA 19063.

Mitchell, J.T. and Everly, G.S. (1993). Critical Incident Stress Debriefing (CISD): an Operations Manual for the Prevention of Traumatic Stress among Emergency Services and Disaster Workers. Ellicott City, MD: Chevron Publishing.

PRESENTATION: TEAM ORGANIZATION AND MANAGEMENT

TEACHING POINTS

I. Team development

MAIN FACTS TO BE PRESENTED

A. Explore the need for a team

B. Organize a steering committee

C. Multi organizational focus

D. Multi jurisdictional focus

E. Review established guidelines

F. Assure mental health involved

G. Gain administrative approval

H. Assure peer involvement

I. Inform organizations

J. Set up team training

II. Team training   Choose instructor (s)

III. Team structure   A. Clinical Director

           B. Team Coordinator

           C. Team Liaison

           D. Members:

                law enforcement

                fire services

                emergency medical

                nurses

                physicians

                communications officers

                corrections officials

                park services

                disaster workers

                wild land fire fighters

                search and rescue personnel

                ski patrol

                life flight programs

                life guards

                industrial personnel

                command officers

                hostage negotiators

                military personnel

                           disaster management teams

                           others as required.

            E. Team leader role

            F. Senior peer role

            G. Peer support personnel roles

IV. Team Operations   A. Continuing education

            B. Cross familiarization

            C. Regular meetings

            D. Written protocols

            E. Confidentiality

            F. Avoiding legal pitfalls

            G. Team discipline

            F. Agency relationships

            H. Media relationships

            I. Team building

            J. Coordination of efforts

Breaks are recommended every 1.5 hours

TOPIC 6: TEN BASIC INTERVENTIONS OF CISM (overview)

Time: 60 minutes

Level of Instruction: one, two, and three - Prepare the learner, present the concepts and assist the learners in making applications encourage discussion and questions from the participants. Some applications is concepts is encouraged in this lesson.

Objectives: When the instruction for this lesson is concluded, the learner should be able to:

* List the ten basic interventions of a CISM
* Explain the term "pre incident education"
* Define the meaning of the term "on scene support"
* Define the term "demobilization"
* Describe a demobilization
* Define the term "defusing"
* Describe a defusing
* Define the term "debriefing"
* Describe a debriefing in general terms
* Explain the meaning of the term "individual consult"
* Briefly describe an individual consult
* Explain the importance of significant other support
* Briefly explain follow up services in CISM
* Define the term "specialty debriefing"
* Describe a specialty debriefing
* Explain what is meant by an "informal discussion"

Materials:

 Workbook and / or handouts on:

    Defusings

    Demobilizations

    Spouse and significant other support

    Specialty debriefings

    etc.

Student provided note pads and writing instruments

Equipment: Audio visual equipment as suggested under equipment in topic 1 above. Equipment utilization is according to instructor requirements.

Audio Visual Aids: It is recommended that instructors utilize slides or overhead transparencies to highlight important points in this section.

References:

Textbooks:

Mitchell, J.T. and Everly, G.S. (1993). Critical Incident Stress Debriefing (CISD): An Operations Manual for the Prevention of Traumatic Stress among Emergency Services and Disaster Workers. Ellicott City, MD: Chevron Publishing.

Mitchell, J.T. and Bray, G.P. (1990). Emergency Services Stress: Guidelines for Preserving the Health and Careers of Emergency Services Personnel. Englewood Cliffs, NJ: Brady Company, Prentice Hall Publishers.

Kennedy-Ewing, L. (1987). Operational and Training Guide for the Critical Incident Stress Management Program of Delaware County, Pennsylvania. Media, PA: Department of Human Resources

PRESENTATION: TEN BASIC CISD INTERVENTIONS

TEACHING POINTS	MAIN FACTS TO BE PRESENTED
I. Pre-incident stress	A. Importance of training
	B. Amount of stress training
	C. New recruit stress training

D. In service stress education

E. Topics to be covered:

       nature of stress

       critical incidents

       critical incident stress

       signs and symptoms

       survival strategies

       critical incident stress teams

       calling for help

       utilizing the help

       significant other programs

       follow up services

       debriefings

       etc.

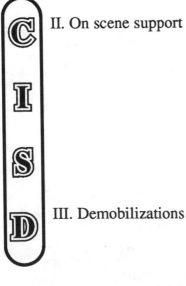

II. On scene support

A. What is it

B. When is it necessary

    1. For prolonged incident

    2. For large scale incident

C. Who calls for it

D. Benefits

III. Demobilizations

A. For large scale events only

B. Transition from big event to routine operations

C. Who does them - trained CISD team members

D. Command endorsement

E. After release from scene only

F. To be followed by debriefing later (3-7 days)

G. Benefits of demobilization

IV. Defusings

A. Definition of defusing

B. Uses of defusings

C. Provided for small core group

D. Shortened version of debriefing

E. May eliminate need for debriefing

F. May enhance debriefing if it is still necessary

V. Debriefings
(CISD)

A. Define CISD

B. Provided by specialized team - mental health and peers

C. Reduces stress reaction

D. Accelerates recovery

E. Seven phases

F. Standard approach

G. Requires training

H. May require follow up

VI. Individual
consults

A. Define individual consult or one on one

B. Who provides - trained CISM team members

C. When necessary - support individuals need

D. Follow up

VII. Significant other support

A. A CISM responsibility

B. Educational programs for significant others

C. Debriefings (CISD) for significant others of emergency operations personnel

D. Bereavement support - grief and crisis counseling

E. Family support - for children, elders

F. Other

VIII. Specialty debriefings

A. Define - for groups outside normal area of responsibility

B. When provided - community is distressed

C. Types of events

D. Level of involvement - limited to avoid too close involvement with citizens

E. Rules for involvement

　　1. Humanitarian reasons

　　2. No fees for service

　　3. No other agencies available in a timely fashion

　　4. Coordination with other agencies

F. Referrals - sometimes necessary

G. Other

IX. Informal discussions

A. Define - leaderless small group conversation about traumatic stress

B. Who is participating - working crew

C. No leader

D. Good diagnostic indicator of stress symptoms

E. Caution signals - high levels of distress

F. Alterations in discussion may occur to render best help to personnel

G. Change into defusing when distress is high and a CISM trained person or two are present

H. Stop the discussion if it has turned very negative or is placing blame on individuals in the group

X. Follow up services A. Define

B. When done - after individual consults, defusings, debriefings, demobilizations, significant other support

C. Who provides - trained CISM personnel

D. Types - telephone calls, station visits, home visits, small group sessions, one on ones, etc.

TOPIC 7: ON SCENE SUPPORT SERVICES

Time: 30 minutes

Level of Instruction: one, two, three and four - Prepare the learner, present the concepts and instruct the learners, encourage discussion and questions from the participants and have the learners evaluate situations and make decisions as to what CISM techniques are most appropriate. In addition, the learners should be required to show that they know how those CISM techniques can be properly applied.

Objectives: Upon completing this topic the student should be able to:

* Define the term on "scene support services"

* Explain at least three approaches to intervening in a fellow workers distress

* Demonstrate the ability to properly intervene on the scene as a peer by answering instructor questions and describing how they would apply on scene support services to emergency personnel in a number of differing circumstances

* Explain the roles and responsibilities of peer support personnel under field conditions

* Describe the circumstances under which mental health professionals on the CISM team might be required at the scene

* Explain the roles and responsibilities of mental health professionals who are called to work with the emergency providers at the scene

* Affirm that no group interventions are ever provided at the scene

* Describe the significant dangers which exist if group interventions are attempted under field conditions.

* List several questions which might be asked of individual emergency personnel by CISM team members supporting them at the scene

* Describe pit falls which are to be avoided by CISM teams at the scene

* List appropriate actions which may be taken by CISM teams

* Explain why removal of emergency personnel from the field of operations is always a last resort.

* Explain why sending an emergency worker home is even more of a last resort than removing the worker from the scene

Materials:

Hand outs related to on scene support

Recommended texts (see topics 1 and 5 above)

Student provided materials for note taking

Equipment: Audio visual equipment as suggested in topic 1

Audio Visual Aids: Slides, brief video tapes, or overhead transparencies are recommended on this topic according to instructor preference and need.

References: It is recommended that the students in a CISD course obtain copies of the reference texts mentioned in topics 1 and 5 above. In addition they should be familiar with the many articles on CIS and CISD which have appeared in the emergency literature over the last decade.

PRESENTATION:

TEACHING POINTS	MAIN FACTS TO BE PRESENTED
I. Team members for on scene support services	A. Choosing members for on scene work
	B. Structuring the response system - reports to whom?

	C. Need for additional training
	    - peer counselor
	    - disaster management

D. Call out system - called as needed

E. Voluntary system - taking turns
   automatic response

II. CIS team
    functions in field

A. Observation of personnel at the
   scene

B. Advice to command staff

C. Support of individuals (groups) showing
   obvious signs of distress

D. Assistance to actual victims of the
   incident and their family members

III. Rules to follow

A. Respect privacy

B. Fulfill first request if possible

C. Work in pairs when possible

D. Only work with individuals,
   never groups at the scene

E. Very brief interventions (5 - 15 maximum)

F. Confidentiality - must be maintained

G. Command approval required whenever
   decisions affect staffing or operations

H. Do not interfere with investigations

I. Use only on significant events

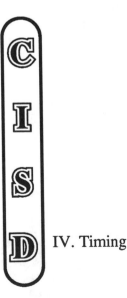

IV. Timing

A. Proximal to scene

B. Immediate intervention

C. Expectant (set expectations for next few

minutes or remainder of operation)

V. Assessment

    A. Obvious signs of distress

    B. Subtle signs of distress

    C. Know the person

    D. Be familiar with cognitive, physical, emotional and behavioral signs and symptoms of distress

    E. Listen to reports from person's colleagues

VI. Interventions

    A. Approach tactfully

    B. Opening remarks

    C. Listening skills

    D. Open ended questions

    E. Statements

    F. Acceptance

    G. Feedback

    H. Privacy

    I. Being discrete

    J. Use of humor

    K. Backing off

    L. Avoiding personal issues

    M. Reassuring

    N. Encouraging

O. Orienting

P. Problem solving

Q. Suggesting

R. Guiding

S. Closing

T. Resting

U. Restoring

V. Rechecking

W. Maintaining gains

X. Lowering stress

Y. Planning next steps

Z. Referring if necessary

VII. Mental Health
professionals
in the field

A. Rules of response:

- do not respond unless called

- cautious response

- report into command

- work under safety officer

- stay out of internal perimeter

- keep a low profile

- do not talk to the media

- work *only* with individuals in distress, *not* groups

- do not get physically involved in the incident

B. Safety consciousness

C. Advise command staff

D. Support for *Individuals*

E. Assist victims, survivors and
their families

F. Establish a demobilization center

G. Staff the demobilization center

H. Think out strategy for demobilizations,
debriefings and follow up sessions

BREAKS ARE RECOMMENDED EVERY 1.5 HOURS

NOTE: THE USE OF AUDIO VISUAL AIDS AND QUES-
TIONS FROM THE AUDIENCE MAY NECESSITATE AN AL-
TERATION IN THE TIME FRAMES PRESENTED IN THIS
COURSE OUTLINE. TIMES SHOWN ONLY SUGGEST THE
MINIMUM TIME NECESSARY TO PRESENT THE BASIC CON-
CEPTS DESCRIBED IN THIS OUTLINE. THEY DO NOT RE-
FLECT THE USE OF AUDIO VISUAL AIDS OR THE MANAGE-
MENT OF QUESTIONS.

TOPIC 8: DEFUSINGS

Time: 45 minutes

Level of Instruction: one, two, three and four - Prepare the learner,
present the basic concepts of defusing. Instruct the learners in using
the techniques associated with defusing. Encourage listener questions and discussion. Provide a demonstration of the defusing
technique in which students play roles such as helper and those in
a group to be helped. Evaluate their performance by observation
and comment.

Objectives: After this lesson, the learners should be able to:

* Define the term "Defusing"

* Describe the differences between "Demobilization", "Defusing" and "Debriefing"

* Understand the best times to utilize a defusing

* Explain the goals of a defusing

* Explain the nature of an event which would necessitate a defusing

* List the three main parts of a defusing

* Recite a typical list of questions which would be asked in a defusing

* State clearly the usual time frame in which the defusing should be performed (time from the event)

* State clearly the usual length of time for the defusing (defusings only last 20-45 minutes)

* Demonstrate, by means of a role play, that the learner has the ability to apply some of the basic defusing concepts presented in the lecture

Materials:

Handouts on Defusings

Texts: (See recommendations under topics 1 and 5 above)

Equipment: Audio visual equipment as suggested under equipment in topic 1 above. Four to six Chairs for the demonstration defusing.

Audio Visual Aids: It is recommended that instructors utilize slides or overhead transparencies to highlight important points in this section.

References: This text and the texts suggested in topics 1 and 5 above.

PRESENTATION:

TEACHING POINTS	MAIN FACTS TO BE PRESENTED
I. Definition	A. Shortened version of debriefing
	B. Group intervention after trauma
	C. Designed to lessen critical incident stress
II. Compare / Contrast to Demobilization and Debriefing	A. Define demobilization
	B. Define Debriefing
	C. Describe the similarities and differences between and among these types of interventions
	D. Note that all three are group interventions after trauma
III. Times	A. Defusing is ideal when provided within 8 hours of the incident
	B. Defusings ordinarily last only 20-45 minutes
IV. Goals	A. Lessen impact
	B. Screen the group for possible further intervention
	C. Restore to normal duties
	D. Prepare the worker to return home with a lighter emotional burden
	E. Eliminate the need to provide a debriefing

F. Enhancement of a debriefing if one is still necessary

V. Triggering events

A. Not an ordinary event

B. An emotionally distressing event

C. A high power event

D. Significant event at beginning of shift

E. Significant event at end of shift

VI. Components

A. Introduction

B. Exploration

C. Information

VII. Suggested questions

A. What happened?

B. Tell me a bit more

C. What was that like for you?

D. What other things were going on?

E. What other details would you like to discuss?

F. What part are you having the most difficulty with right now?

VIII. Demonstration

A. Pick volunteers form audience

B. Provide roles according to a preset scenario

C. Peers defuse others involved in the "incident"

D. Demonstration lasts about 15 minutes

F. Discuss the process / questions

TOPIC 9: DEMOBILIZATIONS

Time: 15 minutes

Level of Instruction: one two and three - Prepare the learner, present the concepts and instruct the learners and encourage discussion and questions from the participants.

Objectives: Upon completing this topic, the learner should be able to:

* Define a demobilization

* Describe the structure and functions of a demobilization center

* Explain how the demobilization works

* Describe the purposes of a demobilization

* Explain the basic rules of a demobilization

Materials:

Handouts on demobilizations

This text and the texts recommended in topics 1 and 5

Student provided materials for note taking

Equipment: Audio visual equipment as required by the instructor

Audio Visual Aids: Slides or overhead transparencies are usually utilized when instructing on this topic.

References: See the recommended texts in topics 1 and 5 above.

PRESENTATION:

TEACHING POINTS	MAIN FACTS TO BE PRESENTED
I. Definition of demobilization	A. Group intervention
	B. After disaster or other large scale incident
	C. Ten minute talk providing information on Critical Incident Stress
	D. Twenty minutes for eating and resting
	E. Transition from the terrible event back to routine
II. Structure of center	A. Two large rooms
	B. One room for information talks
	C. One room for food and rest
	D. Chairs in information room arranged in small circles just large enough to handle the number of workers in each work team
III. Functions of center	A. Information
	B. Rest before return to routine
	C. Nourishment
IV. Goals	A. Lower disaster related stress
	B. Aim personnel toward recovery
	C. **NOT** psychotherapy
V. Staff	A. Mental health professionals

B. Chaplains

C. Off duty CISD trained peers not physically capable of work because of previous injury or not on duty for the disaster

VI. Methods

A. All personnel are sent to demobilization center when they are released from any further work at the disaster

B. Each functional unit (truck company, engine company, tactical team, special unit, etc.) is given its own demobilization

C. Maximum ten minute informative talk on Critical Incident Stress is presented to all workers

D. Demobilizations are not given if the personnel are going to be returned to the same scene

E. Personnel are given an opportunity to ask any questions they wish

F. Personnel may make any statements they wish, but *they do **not** have to speak*

G. Ten minute talk informs the personnel about CIS and suggests numerous helpful hints to assist personnel

H. Personnel then sent to food room if they have no questions or wish not to talk

I. Nutritious foods are supplied

J. Personnel are then returned to normal duties or discharged to home as the commanders decide

TOPIC 10: QUESTIONS AND ANSWERS - TOPICS 1-9

(may be optional if questions have been asked during presentation of topics)

Time: 15 minutes

Level of Instruction: three and four - Encourage discussion and questions from the participants and have the learners apply the concepts to their own situations. Evaluate the effectiveness of the instruction to this point and determine need for remedial instruction before moving on in the material.

Objectives: At the close of this portion of the instruction the learners should be able to:

* Formulate their questions related to the previous topics

* Obtain answers to the majority of their questions

* Participate actively in discussions regarding topics 1-9

* Make preliminary applications of their growing CIS knowledge base in to their own experiences

* Demonstrate and understanding of the information provided

Materials: None required in this session

Equipment: None required in this session

Audio Visual Aids: None required in this session

References: This text and the references listed in all previous topics.

PRESENTATION:

TEACHING POINTS	MAIN FACTS TO BE PRESENTED
I. Encourage questions	A. Accurately answer the questions
	B. Do not provide answers without certainty that the answers are correct
	C. Use examples to illustrate points
II. Ask questions	A. To assess learner absorption of the material
	B. Clarify details
	C. Eliminate confusion
	D. Open up lines of communication
III. Encourage participants to discuss their own applications of the information	A. Assess learner's ability to apply concepts
	B. Eliminate confusion

Note: Since the amount of material is extensive and this material is presented on the afternoon of the first day, a break at this time is important even if the 1.5 hour limit has not been reached. Fifteen to twenty minutes is recommended for a break. This is a natural break point between the material which has already been presented and the material yet to come in the following sessions.

TOPIC 11: DEBRIEFING VIDEO - "TECHNIQUES OF DEBRIEFING"

Time: 45 minutes

Level of Instruction: one - to prepare the mind and set the foundation

Objectives: At the conclusion of this session, the learner will able to:

* Provide a preliminary definition of the term debriefing

* List the seven major phases of a debriefing

* Describe how peer support personnel and mental health professionals interacted as part of the same team during the debriefing

* Have a visual and auditory image of a debriefing

Materials:

      Articles on debriefing

      Texts (This book and those described in topics 1 and 5)

      Student provided note pads and writing instruments

Equipment: 1/2 inch VHS video tape player and television monitor(s) sufficient for the size of the group.

Audio Visual Aids: The video tape, "CISD, Critical Incident Stress Debriefing: Techniques of Debriefing" which is hosted by Dr. Jeffrey T. Mitchell and which has been produced by American Safety Video Publishers, Inc. of Naples, Florida.

References: See suggestions in topics 1 and 5 above.

PRESENTATION:

TEACHING POINTS   MAIN FACTS TO BE PRESENTED

I. Introduction	A. Briefly explain what the video is about
	B. Describe the objectives
II. Play video "CISD"	
III. Accept questions	A. Accept questions
	B. Summary comments

TOPIC 12: OVERVIEW OF THE DEBRIEFING PROCESS

Time: 60 minutes

Level of Instruction: one, two, three and four - Prepare the learner, present the concepts and instruct the learners. Encourage discussion and questions from the participants. Assist the learners in making applications of the concepts to real world situations. Question the learners to asses their absorption of the material.

Objectives: At the conclusion of this session, the learner should be able to:

* Clearly and accurately define a debriefing

* Explain the fact that a debriefing is not psychotherapy

* Cite the indications that a debriefing is necessary

* List the seven phases of a debriefing

* Explain the goals of a debriefing

* Know the average length of time of a debriefing

* Describe the most ideal time for a debriefing

* Understand that a debriefing is a group intervention

* Explain the make up of a CISD team

* Explain what activities must take place before the debriefing occurs

* Explain what activities must take place after the debriefing is concluded

* Know that a debriefing is only provided for an unusually painful event

* Know the basic questions which are asked during a debriefing

Materials:

  Handouts on debriefings

  Recommended texts such as those mentioned in topics 1 and 5 above

  Student provided note taking materials

Equipment: Audio Visual equipment as required by the instructor

Audio Visual Aids: Slides or overhead transparencies are recommended for this topic.

References: This text and those recommended in topics 1 and 5 above.

PRESENTATION:

TEACHING POINTS	MAIN FACTS TO BE PRESENTED
I. Definition	A. Post trauma group meeting
	B. Discussion
	C. **NOT** psychotherapy
	D. Developed for emergency personnel but applicable to many other groups
	E. Psychologically supportive

intervention

F. Educational intervention

II. Goals and objectives   A. Mitigate stress response

B. Accelerate recovery

III. Best time   A. Between 24 and 72 hours is ideal

B. Earlier in some extraordinary cases

C. Later when the requirements of the situation warrant later intervention

D. Loses effectiveness with increased time from the incident

IV. Basic rules   A. Only provided by a team

B. A team for emergency personnel must have both peer support personnel and mental health professionals

C. Team for other than emergency personnel should have at least two trained mental health professionals

D. CISD lasts 2.5 to 3.0 hours on the average

E. Seven phases should be followed

F. Event should be significant

G. Avoid psychotherapy

H. Peers play active role for an emergency services debriefing

I. **Never** done on scene

J. Minimum team is two

K. No one is required to speak

L. Not all the work can be done in a debriefing

M. Use a debriefing when:

- Significant changes in behavior in group

- Regression to less effective performance

- Symptoms continue

- Symptoms intensify

- Group wide symptoms

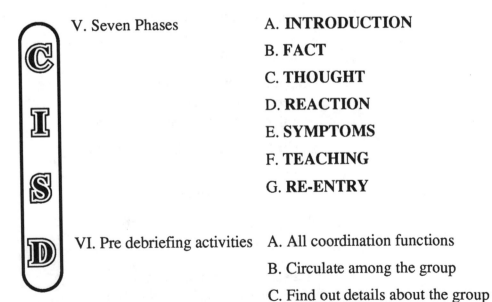

V. Seven Phases

A. **INTRODUCTION**

B. **FACT**

C. **THOUGHT**

D. **REACTION**

E. **SYMPTOMS**

F. **TEACHING**

G. **RE-ENTRY**

VI. Pre debriefing activities

A. All coordination functions

B. Circulate among the group

C. Find out details about the group

D. Review the case

E. Strategy meeting with the team

VII. Post debriefing activities   A. One on One contacts

B. Post debriefing team meeting

C. Post action report

VIII. Usual questions   A. Fact phase -

Who are you?

What was your job in the incident?

What happened?

B. Thought phase -

What was your first thought after you got out of the auto pilot mode?

C. Reaction phase -

What was the worst thing about this event for you?

D. Symptoms phase -

What cognitive, physical, emotional, and behavioral symptoms did you experience at the scene?

Next few days?

Left over now?

E. Teaching phase -

Was there one thing which happened which helped you or made the situation a bit easier to tolerate?

F. Re-entry phase-

Are there any questions you might want to ask?

Any statements anyone would like to make?

Anything else?

This is usually the end of the first day of training. Extensive questions from the audience during the day may cause alterations in the actual time necessary to present the material. Some adjustments may need to be made in the schedule if this is the case.

STANDARD CISD LESSON PLANS

DAY TWO : LESSONS THIRTEEN TO SIXTEEN

TOPIC 13: DEBRIEFING DETAILS

Time: 60 minutes

Level of Instruction: one, two, three and four - Prepare the learner. present the concepts and instruct the learners. Encourage questions and discussion from the learners. Cite examples which assist the learners to make applications of the concepts to real world situations. Question the participants to see if they have properly absorbed the information.

Objectives: At the close of this portion of the instruction the learners should be able to:

* Explain how groups are targeted for debriefings

* Describe the tasks associated with a CISD

* State specific activities to be performed before the CISD

* Detail the introductory remarks made in a debriefing

* State the questions used in the seven CISD phases

* Describe the alternate questions to be used in larger groups during the fact phase of the debriefing

* Explain the alternate method of presenting the thought phase in a CISD

* Describe specifically what is achieved in the re-entry phase of the debriefing

* Describe in detail the post debriefing activities

* Explain in detail the main considerations in the structure and design of the debriefing and its environment

* Explain when follow up services are required

* Describe various types of follow up services

Materials:

Handouts on debriefings

Recommended texts such as those mentioned in topics 1 and 5 above

Student provided note taking materials

Equipment: Audio Visual equipment as required by the instructor

Audio Visual Aids: Slides or overhead transparencies are recommended for this topic.

References: This text and those recommended in topics 1 and 5 above.

NOTE: At times, it will be necessary to alter the order in which the material in the basic CISD training course is presented. This is especially so if the group being trained asks many questions. It is important, however, to keep this lesson before the debriefing demonstration in lesson 14.

PRESENTATION:

TEACHING POINTS	MAIN FACTS TO BE PRESENTED
I. Targeting groups	A. Geography
	B. Function
	C. Arrival time
II. Tasks of CISD	A. Education
	B. Emotional ventilation
	C. Reassurance
	D. Forewarning
	E. Reduce the fallacy of uniqueness
	F. Reduce the fallacy of abnormality
	G. Positive contact with mental health
	H. Increase group cohesiveness
	I. Enhance interagency cooperation
	J. Prevention of PTSD and other stress related problems

K. Screening

L. Referral opportunity

III. Coordination activities   A. Chose date, time, place

B. Check and chose room

C. Make appropriate announcements

D. Invite all involved in incident

E. Gain cooperation of administration and command

F. Arrange for refreshments

G. Arrange fill-ins for personnel

H. Choose CISD team

I. Arrange team transportation

J. Arrange team meeting time

IV. Pre-debriefing activities   A. Divide up team and greet participants as they arrive

B. Gather information which is important to know for debriefing

     - relationship with command

     - relationships to one another

     - unusual circumstances

     - little known but useful facts about incident which might not be stated in the CISD

     - etc.

C. Case review

- scene

- pictures

- incident report

- news papers

- video tapes

- verbal accounts

- other

D. CISD team strategy meeting

- assign roles

- assign positions

- review key points of

  case review

- clarify leadership

- assign general teaching
  duties

- other

V. Introductory remarks
(made by CISD team)

A. Introduce the team leader

B. Point out team members (they
introduce themselves during
the "Fact" phase not now)

C. Ask if anyone doesn't belong in
group

D. Handle those who do not belong

E. Explain the purpose of the meeting

F. Describe what a debriefing is

G. Motivate participants

H. Manage resistance

I. Explain what will happen

J. Ask for any questions

K. Provide reassurances about their concerns

L. Announce the first set of questions to come

M. Encourage mutual help

N. Explain the rules of CISD

    - confidentiality

    - speak for one self

    - people do not have to speak

    - do not leave and not return

    - no breaks

    - participants may leave for bathroom use only

    - no cameras, notes, recordings

    - put aside rank for the CISD

    - not a critique of incident

    - personnel not to respond to calls

    - turn off pagers / radios

    - not investigative

    - do not discuss protocol

violations

- do not discuss criminal behavior

- CISD team is for support only

- other as circumstances require

VI. Fact phase questions
(usually asked to each participants)

A. Who are you?

B. What role did you have in the incident?

C. What happened?

VII. Alternate Fact questions
(not everyone has to speak)

A. Used when there is a group larger than 25

B. Used when there is an unusual time constraint placed on CISD team

C. Instead of:
who are you?
what was your role?
what happened?

Ask:

which units arrived first?

what happened?

who came next?

what happened?

D. Once 6 to 8 people have answered move to next CISD phase

VIII. Thought phase inquiries
(usually asked to each participant)

A. What was your first thought once you got off the auto pilot mode? or

B. What was your main thought during the incident? or

C. What was the most prominent thought as you handled the situation?

IX. Alternate Thought phase **(not everyone has to speak)**

A. Used when group is larger than 25 people

B. Used when time is limited

C. Instead of a question like:

What was your main thought once you got off the auto pilot mode?

Ask:

what were some of you thinking during the incident?

X. Reaction Phase questions

A. What was the very worst thing about this incident for you personally?

B. What part of this experience would you like to erase if it were possible to do so?

C. What part of this event was the most difficult for you or caused you the most distress?

D. Etc.

XI. Symptom phase questions (only those who wish to speak others may remain silent)

A. What were the signals of distress or signs and symptoms of stress you encountered while working at the scene?

- cognitive

- physical

- emotional

- behavioral

B. What types of symptoms did you encounter in the next few days?

- cognitive

- physical

- emotional

- behavioral

C. Do you have any left over symptoms now?

- cognitive

- physical

- emotional

- behavioral

XII. Teaching phase

A. Provided by CISD team members

**(CISD team does most
of the work)**

B. Standard topics addressed

- diet
- exercise
- rest
- alcohol
- drugs
- contact with family
- contact with friends
- group social network
- symptoms mentioned in session
- other symptoms not mentioned
- calling for help if necessary
- long range effects of stress
- when to call for help
- recovery is typical
- debriefings may cause some initial pain, but there is more pain without them

C. Customized topics

- address the needs of the group
- answer concerns and questions
- touch upon the CISD themes
- other

XIII. Re-entry phase

(Both participants and CISD team interact. No participant speaks unless he or she wants to talk. Only the CISD members make a summary comment)

A. Participants:

- ask any questions they have
- may go back over information and issues already discussed in the session

- may bring up new material not previously discussed
- may bring up other issues if necessary

B. CISD team members:

- provide additional information and reassurance
- may have to state, in a general sense, feelings and thoughts which the participants are unwilling or unable to discuss but the team suspects may be present.
- provide handout material to the participants
- each CISD team member makes a brief summary comment designed to encourage or reassure the group

XIV. Post debriefing activities A. CISD team immediately starts
(Done by CISD team alone)   making contact with those from
                                   the session who seem to need
                                   additional support.

- a few words

- a brief one-on-one

- a referral if needed

- a special meeting with the
  team leader

- etc.

B. Post debriefing meeting

a. Review the debriefing and
try to learn something
from it. Make educational
points for the team members.

b. Decide on who is going to
provide the follow up
services. Determine which
kinds of follow up will be
necessary.

c. Most important! Debrief
the debriefing team. The
CISD team needs to
ventilate. Make sure
everyone is okay before
sending the team home.

C. Post action report (optional)

a. one paragraph describing
the event.

b. one paragraph describing the important themes or issues which came up (but do not write anything which could identify a specific participant).

c. one paragraph which describes the types of suggestions and support given by the team.

d. cite names of CISD team members, date of debriefing, number of participants present.

e. only used for team records and training.

Not for any other purpose.

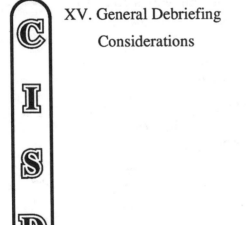

XV. General Debriefing Considerations

A. Location

- quiet room

- movable furniture

- big enough room for group

- carpeted

- dimmable lights

- air conditioned or

- heated

- one access door

- no phone interruptions

- comfortable seats

- radio speakers turned off

B. Time

- convenient to majority

C. Invite all involved personnel

D. Personnel relieved of response duties

E. No media, recorders, cameras

F. No uninvolved personnel

G. No citizens (separate CISD for them)

H. No spectators

I. No non emergency significant others

J. Not mixed with operations critique

K. CISD is not a critique

L. No breaks of process

M. Strict confidentiality for all

N. More than 4 people

O. 4-20 people is ideal

P. 20-30 reasonably comfortable

Q. 30-40 people - split group or change procedure to alternate question format

R. Avoid going above 40 people

S. Target primary populations

T. Usual CISD response team size

    4-10 people - 2 CISD

    11-20 people - 3-4 CISD

    21- 30 people - 5 CISD

    31-40 people - 6 CISD

U. Debriefings should always be followed up

XVI. Follow up Services

A. Always necessary after:
- one-on-one contact (individual consult)
- demobilization
- defusing
- debriefing

B. Especially necessary after a debriefing

C. Types of follow up:
- phone calls
- station visits
- individual consults
- peer visits
- home visits
- chaplain visits
- ride along
- brief follow up group

meeting one week later

- calls / visits initiated by the individual

- checking with command staff

- other

TOPIC 14: DEBRIEFING DEMONSTRATION

Time: 2 - 2.5 hours

Level of Instruction: one, two, three, four - All of the instructor's teaching and clinical skills will be brought together during this most important aspect of the training program. It will be necessary to prepare the learner, but somewhat less emphasis will be placed on the presentation of concepts. What is emphasized is the interaction, questions and discussion from the learners and a demonstration of the skills previously taught. This segment of the training allows the instructor to demonstrate real world applications of the material and it also affords a good opportunity for the instructor to determine if the instruction has been effective.

Objectives: At the conclusion of this demonstration the learner should be able to:

* Observe a properly run debriefing demonstration

* React to situations, questions and interactions which occur during the demonstration debriefing

* Explain how the debriefing process differs substantially from group psychotherapy

* Describe how the seven phases of the debriefing link together

Materials: No special materials are required for the debriefing demonstration. Observers should have their notebooks and pens available.

Equipment: The debriefing demonstration requires enough chairs in a circle to accommodate between 10 and 15 role players who will be playing out the role of a group needing a debriefing. There should be sufficient chairs for a "CISD team" of 3 to 4 "debriefers".

Audio Visual Aids: No audio visual equipment is necessary unless the room and the audience is very large. In that case a microphone or several microphones might be necessary.

References: This text and those recommended in topics 1 and 5 above.

PRESENTATION:

TEACHING POINTS	MAIN FACTS TO BE PRESENTED
I. Decide upon a scenario	A. Select a scenario that meets the needs of the group
	B. Pick a scenario for an event which would be powerful enough to require a debriefing if it were real
	C. Choose a fictitious event, but one which has some basis in reality (a believable event)
II. Choose volunteers for roles	A. Pick the number of volunteers necessary to handle the roles
	B. People should play the same or nearly the same roles they hold in real life
	C. Choose 2 to 4 "debriefers".

Experienced real life debriefers
are an asset

D. Carefully brief the role players

E. Put into the role some situations
which tend to happen in actual
debriefings

- someone departs upset and the
doorkeeper has to retrieve that
person

- a pager goes off in the thought
phase

- one who stays silent throughout
most of the "debriefing" only to
tell a big secret in the teaching
phase

- one who is angry about being in
the debriefing in the introduction
phase and who has to be talked
into staying

- one who feels very guilt ridden
and blames oneself for the tragedy

F. Brief the "CISD team" for their
important role in the demonstration

III. Prepare the learners

A. Set the circle of chairs in the
middle of the room

B. Place the observers all around
the circle

C. Provide a brief verbal description
of the "incident"

D. Advise the group how the demonstration works

E. Show how and why the group is arranged

F. Ask if there are any questions from the audience

G. Ask the observers to stay out of the debriefing scenario while it is ongoing, but encourage the observers to ask questions when the demonstration goes into a "freeze frame" mode periodically during the demonstration

H. Give last minute introductory remarks and final instructions

IV. Manage demonstration

A. Plan to "freeze frame" the demonstration after the introduction and fact phases have been completed

B. If something highly unusual occurs during the demonstration, go into an immediate "freeze frame" and discuss the occurrence with the audience. Then resume the demonstration

C. Follow the seven phase process

D. The second "freeze frame" occurs after the thought phase and the reaction phase have been completed

E. The longest "freeze frame" usually takes place after the reaction phase. This discussion includes the management of one who departs from the group as well as any other unusual situations.

F. The last three phases, symptoms, teaching and re-entry are taken together without a "freeze frame"

G. The last three phases and general questions are managed after the demonstration is concluded

H. A demonstration debriefing which goes from the beginning to the end without "freeze frames" can be educationally careless and psychologically dangerous. People would have too many concepts being demonstrated to them far too quickly for proper absorption. They would lose out on opportunities to have their questions answered while they are still fresh. No "freeze frames" in a demonstration debriefing may allow the demonstration to become too intense by stirring up too many old feelings. The "freeze frames" blocks the intensity and keeps the demonstration educational and interrupts the tendency for the demonstration to turn into a real debriefing.

The second day lunch break usually occurs at this point. It should also be noted that the morning break usually occurs in between topics 13 and 14. It is a somewhat longer break which allows time for the demonstration volunteers to be prepared for their roles. No other formal break is taken during the demonstration debriefing those observing the demonstration are free to leave the room for their own breaks if needed during the demonstration.

At times, the demonstration debriefing occurs in the afternoon of the second day because other material may take longer to present. This arrangement is fine as long as the entire demonstration can be completed.

The demonstration debriefing usually includes some of the problem situations which may occur in a real debriefing. This may include a person who departs during the debriefing, a pager going off during the session, a person who is verbally resistant to participating in the debriefing and other problems which must be addressed by the debriefing team. The demonstration organizers should be careful not to overdo these "problem" cases or the demonstration will become exceedingly difficult to manage and the observers will begin to focus excessively on the difficulties of debriefing rather than on the debriefing process.

TOPIC 15: QUESTION AND ANSWER PERIOD

Time: 30 minutes

Level of instruction: three and four - Encourage additional discussion and questions from the participants. The debriefing demonstration usually generates a great many questions and every effort should be made to answer as many of these questions as possible. Some questions may be asked of the audience in an effort to have the participants apply the concepts they have learned to their own experiences.

Objectives: At the completion of this portion of the instruction the learners should be able to:

* Express their questions related to the debriefing demonstration and real debriefings

* Obtain answers to the majority of their questions

* Participate actively in discussions relevant to the debriefing demonstration and debriefings in general

* Make applications of CISD concepts to their own experiences

* Verbally demonstrate their understanding of the information provided in the previous topics

Materials: None required in this session

Equipment: Blackboard or flip chart may be helpful to clarify certain points.

Audio Visual Aids: None except that note in the equipment section above is necessary during this session.

References: This text and the references listed in all previous topics.

PRESENTATION:

TEACHING POINTS	MAIN FACTS TO BE PRESENTED
I. Encourage questions	A. Accurately answer the questions
	B. Do not provide answers without certainty that the answers are correct
	C. Use examples to illustrate points
II. Ask questions	A. To assess learner absorption the material
	B. Clarify details
	C. Eliminate confusion
	D. Open lines of Communication
III. Encourage participants	A. Assess learner's ability to apply

to discuss their
own applications
of the information

concepts
B. Eliminate confusion

TOPIC 16: UNFINISHED BUSINESS / FINAL QUESTIONS AND ANSWERS /COURSE CONCLUSION

Time: 1 to 1.5 hours

Level of Instruction: one, two, three, and four - Prepare the learner, present the concepts, instruct the learners and encourage discussion and questions fro the participants. Assist the learners in making applications of the concepts to real world situations. Question the learners to assess their absorption of the material.

Objectives: At the conclusion of this session, the learner should be able to:

* Understand the fine points of debriefings

* Understand the interactions of debriefing team members

* Apply basic debriefing concepts in coordination with their own CIS management team

* Obtain answers to their final questions

* Know the next steps they are to take either to join an existing CISM team or to formulate one in their own areas

Materials: None needed for this segment of the course

Equipment: None necessary for this segment of the course

Audio Visual Aids: None necessary to present this final information unless the instructor(s) is using slides or overheads to summarize the final statements.

References: This text and those recommended in topics 1 -15 above.

PRESENTATION:

TEACHING POINTS	MAIN FACTS TO BE PRESENTED
I. Summary points on debriefings	A. Discuss any points not yet made B. Encourage questions
II. Final points on uses and abuses of CISD	A. Ask participants questions to assure that they understand the concepts presented B. Clarify any points of confusion
III. Reemphasize the team approach in CISD	A. Discuss team interactions B. Remind the group of post debriefing meeting C. Remind the learner to provide follow up after debriefing
IV. Discuss the next steps for the participants	A. What currently exists B. How to get involved C. Getting started
V. Final questions	A. Accept final questions B. Answer questions accurately
VI. Concluding remarks	A. Acknowledgments B. Thank you's

C
I
S
D

Page 197

C. Farewell remarks

NOTE: The local existing CISM teams frequently participate in the concluding session to insure that the participants know what to do after the course is completed.

Reminder: No one should attempt to teach this course unless they hold the proper credentials and have the right kinds of experience. Please refer to the guidelines in the beginning of chapter four to review the guidelines for instructor qualifications to teach this material.

CHAPTER 7

Issues in Empirical Research Design

INTRODUCTION

The majority of this text is dedicated to issues relevant to training, specifically, teaching the critical incident stress debriefing (CISD) intervention to those who will be using the CISD at a "basic" or "entry" level.

As the field of traumatic stress management has expanded over the last decade, it has become clear that "refinements" and alterations have become necessary, e.g., school-based CISD, mass disaster CISD, etc. The need for, and development of, these refinements has been empirically driven in naturalistic settings. They have not been merely exercises in theoretical nor academic confabulation. Nevertheless, the entire field of traumatic stress management may well benefit from further refinements in the overall process of empirical discovery. Therefore, we have decided to take this opportunity to make a few comments relevant to the design of controlled empirical research as it may relate to CISD or CISM.

THE DESIGN PROCESS

There exist five fundamental steps in the overall design of empirical research:

1) Creation of a research question;

2) Development of a research hypothesis;

3) Selection of measurement tools designed to measure relevant variables;

4) Development of a <u>research design</u>; and

5) <u>Data analyses</u> and <u>conclusion</u> formulation.

These processes apply to the design of empirical research whether it is to be conducted upon CISD, teaching technologies, pharmacologic interventions, or any other area of interest wherein cause and effect relationships are likely to be pursued. While acknowledging that entire textbooks may be written on any one of these 5 processes alone, let's take a closer look at each of them as they might be relevant to empirical research in critical incident stress management.

CREATION OF A RESEARCH QUESTION

Research typically begins with a question for which there is someone who seeks an answer. For example: "Does CISD work?" or, "Is CISD effective?".

While a useful starting point, it should be clear that simply asking the question in such a manner leaves the pursuit of knowledge in far too vague a condition. Greater specificity is needed.

DEVELOPMENT OF A RESEARCH HYPOTHESIS

The research hypothesis is the researcher's opportunity to more concretely operationalize the research question. Yet the hypothesis goes beyond the question and becomes a proposal, or statement, regarding the existence of a relationship between two or more factors, or variables. The relationship may be: 1) cause and effect (causal), or 2) correlational (sequential or contemporaneous but not casual). Of course, there may be no relationship whatsoever between the variables.

Thus, the job of the hypothesis is to bring the research question one step closer to being answered. For example:

RESEARCH QUESTION: "Is CISD effective?"

RESEARCH HYPOTHESIS: "The CISD process will prove effective in reducing stress after a traumatic, critical incident."

It should be clear that the hypothesis is a clearer conceptualization as well as operationalization of the conduct of inquiry vis-a-vis the effectiveness of the CISD process.

SELECTION OF MEASUREMENT TOOLS

"In the final analysis, the empirical basis of epistemology is measurement." The selection of the measurement tools or technologies is often thought of as the Achilles' Heel of research. No matter how powerful one's research design and data analyses may be, if the researcher has failed to choose the appropriate measurement instruments, the study may be an exercise in futility.

The question arises as to just what the researcher actually measures. The answer is "variables". Variables fall into several fundamentally recognized categories:

1. Independent Variables (sometimes called manipulated, treatment or input variables) are factors assumed to cause, affect, or otherwise directly influence some outcome. The outcome is the subject of the next category.

2. Dependent Variables (sometimes called outcome or output variables) are the variables or factors that are most commonly measured in response to a change or manipulation in the independent variable.

3. Control Variables (sometimes called organismic or classificatory variables) are variables or factors that presumably need to be held constant neutralized, randomized or otherwise controlled for they represent potentially alternative sources of effect, i.e., they could possibly exert such an influence so as to cause a change in the dependent variable.

These variables are depicted schematically below with relevant examples from CISM (see Figure 1).

In the example in Figure 1 it should be clear that following the exposure to some critical incident (traumatic event) the intervention,

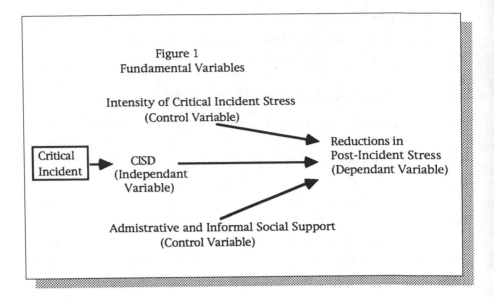

Figure 1
Fundamental Variables

Intensity of Critical Incident Stress
(Control Variable)

Critical
Incident

CISD
(Independant
Variable)

Reductions in
Post-Incident Stress
(Dependant Variable)

Admistrative and Informal Social Support
(Control Variable)

i.e., the independent variable, is the CISD. The manner in which the researcher will assess the effectiveness of the CISD is by measuring the dependent variable, in this case, the changes in acute or long term post-incident stress arousal experienced by the participants of the CISD. It is equally important to note that it is imperative for the researcher to somehow control for phenomena that may confound the effects of the CISD. Two variables that are important to control, or randomize, will be other forms of stress mitigation (e.g. administrative support and informal social support), and even more importantly, the researcher will have to make sure that all subjects in the research study have been exposed to equivalent levels of critical incident (traumatic) stress.

Having reviewed the most fundamental of variables, there remain two other types of variables worth mentioning at this point: antecedent variables and intervening variables.

The antecedent variable exists prior to the independent variable in a causal sequence. The antecedent variable is assumed to be directly responsible for the independent variable which is then assumed to influence the dependent variable. Figure 2 depicts this

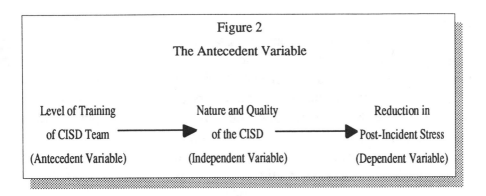

Figure 2

The Antecedent Variable

Level of Training of CISD Team (Antecedent Variable) → Nature and Quality of the CISD (Independent Variable) → Reduction in Post-Incident Stress (Dependent Variable)

relationship. Clearly the level of training of the CISD team will greatly affect the nature and quality of the debriefing itself.

The intervening variable, on the other hand, serves as a variable, or mechanism, by which the independent variable works to ultimately exert an effect upon the dependent variable. Stated another way, the intervening variable is best viewed as a <u>consequence</u> of the independent variable and as a <u>determinant</u> of the dependent variable. Figure 3 depicts this relationship including the antecedent variable.

Figure 3 demonstrates that one possible consequence of the CISD is a catharsis, i.e., a release of emotions. Such a release of emotions may contribute to the reductions of acute post-incident

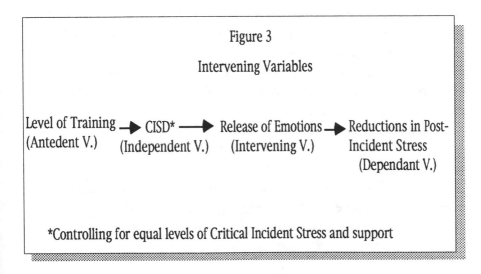

Figure 3

Intervening Variables

Level of Training (Antedent V.) → CISD* (Independent V.) → Release of Emotions (Intervening V.) → Reductions in Post-Incident Stress (Dependant V.)

*Controlling for equal levels of Critical Incident Stress and support

stress.

Having discussed the concept of variables, let us return more directly to the issue of measurement. The variable that is most commonly the target of actual measurement is the dependent variable. In the example above, therefore, the dependent variable to be measured would be the subjective levels of stress reduction experienced by CISD participants as a direct result of the CISD itself.

The critical issue to be addressed by the researcher, therefore, is how to actually measure subjective levels of stress. The answer to this problem is addressed by an integration of two processes:

1) review of valid and reliable psychometric indices of stress, and

2) the design of the research process itself.

There are many sources of valid and reliable measures of subjective stress arousal (and other psychological dimensions) that may be useful for CISD research. Two major sources would be the numerous psychometric test publishers themselves who advertise in various professional journals, or instruments that are published in professional journals as components of scholarly and scientific discourse. When using such tests or assessment instruments it is important to follow the prescribed code of ethics regarding their use. In order to use a test in a manner other than as operationally prescribed, the researcher needs to make note of the nontraditional use and consider interpretation of resultant data in a broader, more flexible context, not considering any conclusions definitive, until supportive data are forthcoming. Table 1 lists several potential dependent variables that can be used in CISD research.

Generally speaking, when selecting the measurement tool in order to measure any of the variables noted above, validity and reliability are the key concepts to address. Validity refers to the demonstrated ability of a test or assessment tool to do that which it purports to be able to do. Reliability refers to the stability or consistency of the measurement tool. Most practically speaking,

Table 1

Potential Dependent (Outcome) Variables

<u>Affective-Cognitive</u>	<u>Behavioral</u>
Subjective stress arousal	Social withdrawal / isolation
Depression	Job performance ratings
Anxiety	Lost work days
Dissociative symptoms	Medical Claims
Hostility	

<u>Physiological</u>

Immunocompetence
Cardiovascular reactivity

consistency over time is the aspect of reliability most often considered, i.e., Does the test perform consistently? Reliability is the sine qua non of all measurement.

RESEARCH DESIGN

The best of all experimental research designs is that which is referred to as the "true experimental design". True experimental designs are those designs in which participants are randomly assigned to groups (experimental and control groups) within the investigative process. The concept and utilization of random assignment provides each participant with an equal opportunity to be placed in either the experimental or control group. True experimental designs allow for the testing of causal processes. Figure 4 depicts the concept of the true experimental design with two groups.

In actual field research it becomes difficult to employ "true experimental designs." As a result, researchers sometimes turn to a

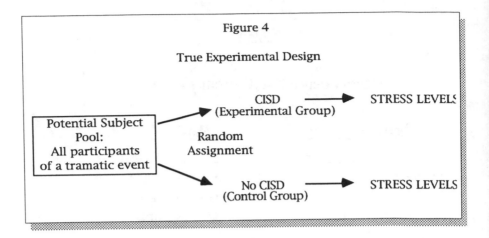

Figure 4

True Experimental Design

Potential Subject
Pool:
All participants
of a tramatic event

Random
Assignment

CISD ⟶ STRESS LEVEL!
(Experimental Group)

No CISD ⟶ STRESS LEVELS
(Control Group)

model that is less powerful in assessing causality, but more practical. That model is called the "quasi-experimental design". The "quasi-experimental" design differs from the "true experimental design" in that the quasi-experimental design fails to employ randomization. Self-selection or naturalistic selection is usually what determines which participants end up in the experimental group versus the control group. Despite this weakness in the design itself, Cook and Campbell (1979) offer methods by which useful data may emerge from the quasi-experimental design. Such a discussion is far beyond the scope of this text, however.

Another aspect of the research design process pertains to the point within the research design where the measuring of variables actually occurs. For the sake of parsimony, we will restrict our comments to the dependent variable. The researcher can measure the dependent variable prior to the experimental intervention in order to establish a baseline. After the intervention, measurements may be once again taken and compared to the baseline. This form of assessment is referred to as the pre-test, post-test within subjects design $(0_1 - 0_2)$. Sometimes researchers will choose not to assess pre-test baseline levels and will perform a post-test only, between subjects design $(0_2 - 0_4)$ assessing the dependent variable between the comparison groups after the intervention. Finally, some researchers conduct

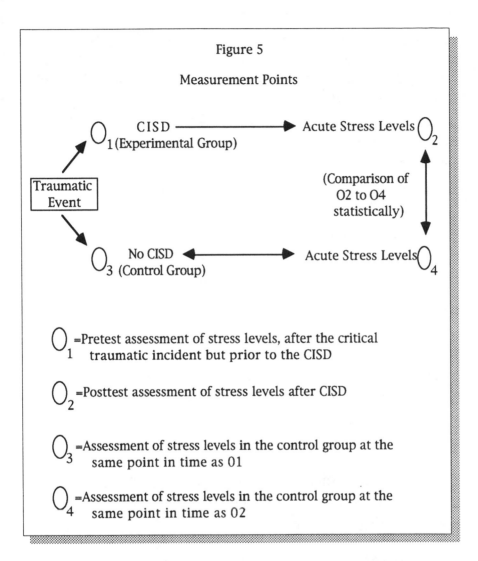

Figure 5

Measurement Points

O_1 CISD ⟶ Acute Stress Levels O_2
(Experimental Group)

Traumatic Event

(Comparison of O2 to O4 statistically)

O_3 No CISD ⟷ Acute Stress Levels O_4
(Control Group)

O_1 =Pretest assessment of stress levels, after the critical traumatic incident but prior to the CISD

O_2 =Posttest assessment of stress levels after CISD

O_3 =Assessment of stress levels in the control group at the same point in time as O1

O_4 =Assessment of stress levels in the control group at the same point in time as O2

both types of measurement analyses within the some investigation. Figure 5 depicts these issues.

In sum, there exist many different types of research designs some with randomization, some without; some with pretesting, some without. The design of the research itself is intended most fundamentally to minimize threats to the integrity of the overall research process.

The integrity of the research process is referred to as <u>internal</u> <u>validity</u>. Thus, in the final analysis all research should be designed with the potential threats to internal validity in mind. The most common threats to internal validity are:

1. History Effect - the occurrence of some event at the same time as the experimental intervention which may change the dependent variable.

2. Maturation Effect - a natural change within subjects with the passage of time, only.

3. Testing Effect - a change in the dependent variable due to pretesting.

4. Instrumentation Effect - problems associated with how the dependent variable is actually measured.

5. Regression Effect - the natural tendency for extreme scores obtained on one testing to regress on subsequent testings.

6. Selection Effect - the use of groups of subjects who are too different at baseline to allow subsequent comparison.

7. Experimental Mortality - subjects dropping out of the study thus biasing the results.

No research design is complete without establishing a checklist to make sure each of these threats to internal validity has been controlled for.

DATA ANALYSES

The final topic of this chapter is data analysis. The manner in which dependent and other variables are routinely analyzed is through a process known as <u>inferential</u> <u>statistical</u> <u>analysis</u>. While the topic is far beyond the scope of this text, a few comments seem relevant.

Statistical analyses assist the researcher in drawing certain conclusions regarding the "power" and "significance" of the findings revealed through the research.

Common statistical procedures used in behavioral science research include the t-test, t-test for correlated means, analysis of variance, analysis of covariance, chi-square analysis, etc. Different tests possess varying levels of discriminating power. Power is also a function of the size of the sample (number of participants). Generally speaking, the larger the sample size, the more powerful the analysis.

Statistical significance is the term used to communicate the likelihood that the results obtained during the study were not obtained due to chance. Statistical significance is expressed in terms of the probability of making an "alpha error". In simple English, an alpha error may be thought of as the eventuality of "discovering something that is not really there". Obviously researchers desire to minimize the likelihood of an alpha error.

In the final analysis, the conclusions the researcher reaches as a result of the research data must possess external validity. External validity is defined as the degree to which the findings revealed by the research are generalizable beyond the sample population to other settings, populations, etc..

There are 4 major jeopardizing factors that compromise external validity:

1. Interaction effects of selection biases and the independent variable. In other words, there may be some characteristic of the sample population that would make the independent variable more effective with the sample yet not other populations.

2. Pretesting interacting with the independent variable. The process of pretesting may actually change the sample population in such a way (e.g., increasing or decreasing sensitivity to the independent variable) so that generalizability to populations which have not been pretested is impossible.

3. Experimental procedures interacting with the independent variable. This is the same type of contamination as in the pretesting interaction where the process of the research itself somehow

changes the sample other than throughout independent variable.

4. Multiple-treatment effects. Similar to the previous two factors, multiple interventions may somehow increase or decrease the sensitivity of the sample population to any independent variable (intervention).

All of these factors limit the generalizability of the findings beyond the specific study itself.

CONCLUSION

This chapter has briefly overviewed the concept of research. We have covered topics relevant to an overview of the design process including 1) the research question, 2) research hypothesis, 3) measurement tools, 4) research design, and 5) data analyses and conclusions.

Clearly, the challenge for CISD researchers, as noted earlier, is finding individuals who have been exposed to the same critical incident (or equivalent critical incidents) who can then be randomly assigned to a CISD intervention group and a NO CISD control group. Given the international acceptance of the CISD intervention, can we ethically withhold the CISD from individuals who desire it? Can we use groups of individuals who "self-select out" i.e. voluntarily choose not to take advantage of the CISD? Will there be a self selection bias?

Such is the dilemma of field research.

Suggested Voluntary Training Standards for Performing Critical Incident Stress Management with Emergency Services, Disaster Response and Humanitarian Aid Personnel

Suggested Training Standards for Peer Support Personnel

A "peer" is defined as a volunteer or paid member of one of the generally recognized emergency service professions, disaster response professions, or humanitarian aid professions. These include, but are not limited to, law enforcement, fire suppression, nursing, emergency medicine, emergency dispatch, chaplaincy, humanitarian aid services, disaster management, search and rescue personnel, ski patrol, life guards, etc.

Recommended Critical Incident Stress Management Training:

1. An entry-level Basic CISD course (2 days minimum)

2. An Advanced CISD course (2 days)

3. A Peer Counseling course (2 days)

4. A Family Support Services course (1 day minimum)

Suggested Training Standards for Mental Health Professionals:

A "mental health professional" is defined as an individual possessing a graduate or professional degree in one of the generally recognized mental health professions, e.g., psychology, counseling, psychiatric nursing, psychiatry, social work and mental health counselors.

Recommended Critical Incident Stress Management Training:

1. An entry-level Basic CISD course (2 days minimum)

2. An Advanced CISD course (2 days)

3. A course on Psychotraumatology and/or the Assessment and Treatment of Post-traumatic Stress Disorder (1 day minimum)

It is clearly acknowledged that these training standards are the "ideal" and should be viewed as voluntary guidelines. Given the infancy of the field of critical incident stress management for emergency response personnel, we recognize that it may be literally years before these standards can be met. Nevertheless, most would agree that emergency response professionals face unique challenges during the pursuit of their career. Those who are dedicated to supporting those professionals must be uniquely trained with the goal of excellence always in mind. By touching the lives of these professionals, one touches not only these professionals themselves and their families, but one has the ability to touch the lives of all who are served by the collective professions we call emergency services, disaster response and humanitarian aid.

REFERENCES

Adkins, L.W. (1991). Making an effective Presentation. Your Company, summer, p.6.

Alexander, D. (1990) Psychological intervention for victims and helpers after disasters. British Journal of General Practice, 40, 345-348.

American Psychiatric Association (1980). Diagnostic and Statistical Manual of Mental Disorders, (Third Edition). Washington, DC: APA Press.

American Psychiatric Association (1987). Diagnostic and Statistical Manual of Mental Disorders, (Third Edition - Revised). Washington, DC: APA Press

Bachtler, J. R. (1989). Fire Instructor's Training Guide, (Second Edition). New York, NY: Fire Engineering.

Billingsley, R. (1993). Fostering Diversity: Teaching by Discussion. The Teaching Professor, 7(2). pp. 3-4.

Cook, T. D. and Campbell, D. T. (1979). Quasi-experimentation. Chicago, IL: Rand McNally.

Corneil, D. W. (1993). Prevalence of Post Traumatic Stress Disorders in a Metropolitan Fire Department. Doctoral Dissertation Baltimore, MD: School of Hygiene and Public Health of Johns Hopkins University

Cummings, N. A. and Vanden Bos, G. (1981). The twenty year Kaiser-Permanente experience with psychotherapy and medical utilization. Health Policy Quarterly, 1, 2-14.

Donovan, D. (1991). Traumatology: A field whose time has come. Journal of Traumatic Stress, 4, 433-436.

Dyregrov, A and Mitchell, J.T. (1992). Working with traumatized children: Psychological effects and coping strategies. Journal of Traumatic Stress, 5(1): 5-17.

Everly, G.S. (1989) A clinical Guide to the Treatment of the Human Stress Response. New York, NY: Plenum

Everly, G.S. (1992) Psychotraumatology. Invited paper presented to the fourth Montreux Congress on Stress. Montreux, Switzerland, February.

Fay, J. (1988). Approaches to Criminal Justice Training. Athens, GA: Carl Vinson Institute of Government, University of Georgia

Federal Emergency Management Agency (FEMA). (1991). Stress Management: Model program for maintaining fire fighter well being. Washington, DC: FEMA, US Fire Administration.

Figley, C. (1993). Forward. In J. Wilson and B. Raphael (Eds.) International Handbook of Traumatic Stress Syndromes. New York, NY: Plenum, pp. xvii-xx.

Freudenheim, M. (1987). Business and health. New York Times, May 26.

Girdano, D.A., Everly, G.S. and Dusek, D.E. (1993) Controlling Stress and Tension: A holistic Approach, fourth edition. Englewood Cliffs, NJ: Prentice Hall.

Hafen, B.Q. and Frandsen, K.J. (1985). Psychological Emergencies and Crisis Intervention: A comprehensive guide for emergency personnel. Englewood, CO: Morton Publishing Company.

Hann, N. (1985). Conceptualizations of ego: Processes, functions, regulations. In A. Monat and R.S. Lazarus, Stress and Coping: an Anthology (Second Edition). New York, NY: Columbia University Press.

Harrison, L.H. (1977). How to teach police subjects: Theory and Practice, (Second Edition). Springfield, MO: Charles C. Thomas Publishers

Hytten, K. and Hasle, A. (1989) Firefighters: A study of stress and coping. Acta Psychiatrica Scandinavica, 80, pp. 50-85.

IFSTA, (1981). Fire Service Instructor. Stillwater, OK: International Fire Service Training Association, Fire protection Publications, Oklahoma State University

Jacobs, L.C. and Chase, C.I. (1992). Developing and Using Tests Effectively: A guide for faculty. San Francisco, CA: Jossey-Bass.

Kliman. A.S. (1978) Crisis: Psychological first aid for Recovery and Growth. Northvale, NJ: Jason Aronson, Inc.

Lang, P. (1971). The application of psychophysiological methods to the study of psychotherapy and behavior modification. In A. Bergin and S. Gargield (Eds.), Handbook of Psychotherapy and Behavior Change. New York, NY: Wiley.

Leeman-Conley, M. (1990). After a violent robbery. Criminology Australia, 4, pp. 4-6.

Life Net staff (1993). The certification issue: where to? Life Net, (published by the International Critical Incident Stress Foundation), 4(2): p.5.

Maslow, A.H. (1954). Motivation and Personality. New York: Harper and Row, Publishers, Inc.

McGee, R. K. (1974). Crisis Intervention in the Community. Baltimore, MD: University Park Press.

Mitchell, J.T. (1983). When disaster strikes...The critical incident stress debriefing process. Journal of Emergency Medical Services 8(1); 36-39.

Mitchell, J.T. (1988)a. The history, status and future of critical incident stress debriefing teams. Journal of Emergency Medical Services. 13(11): 49-52

Mitchell, J.T. (1988)b. Development and functions of a critical incident stress debriefing team. Journal of Emergency Medical

Services. 13(12): 43-46.

Mitchell, J.T. and Bray, G. P. (1990) Emergency Services Stress: Guidelines for preserving the health and careers of emergency services personnel. Englewood Cliffs, NJ: Brady Publishing.

Mitchell, J. T. and Everly, G. S. (1993). Critical Incident Stress Debriefing (CISD): An operations manual for the prevention of traumatic stress among emergency services and disaster workers. Ellicott City, MD: Chevron Publishing Corporation.

Mitchell, J.T. and Resnik, H.L.P. (1981, 1986) Emergency Response to Crisis. Ellicott City, MD: Chevron Publishing Corporation.

Myers, D. (1990) Training Manual for Disaster Mental Health. Sacramento, CA: California Department of Mental Health.

Neff, R.A. and Weimer, M. (Eds.). (1989). Classroom Communication: Collected Readings for Effective Discussion and Questioning Madison, WI: Magna Publications, Inc.

Parad, H.J. (Ed.). (1965). Crisis Intervention: Selected Readings. New York, NY: Family Service Association of America.

Pennebaker, J. and Susman, J. (1988). Disclosure of traumas and psychosomatic processes. Social Science and Medicine, 26, 327 - 332.

Reese, J. T. and Horn, J.M. (Eds) (1988). Police Psychology: Operational assistance. Washington, DC: Federal Bureau of Investigation, US Government printing Office.

Reese, J.T., Horn, J.M. and Dunning, C. (1991). Critical Incidents in Policing, Revised. Washington, DC: US Government Printing Office.

Robinson, R. C. and Mitchell, J.T. (1993). Evaluation of Psychological Debriefings. Journal of Traumatic Stress, 6(3): 367-382.

Rogers, O. (1993). An Examination of the Critical Incident Stress Debriefing for Emergency Personnel: a quasi experimental field survey. University microfilms. Ann Arbor, MI

Schor, J. (1991) The Overworked American. New York, NY: Basic Books.

Simpson, R.D. (1991). Substance versus style: A teaching controversy. Innovative Higher Education, 15(2): 103-107.

van der Hart, O., Brown, P. and van der Kolk, B. (1989). Pierre Janet's treatment of post-traumatic stress. Journal of Traumatic Stress, 2, 379-396.

van der Kolk, B.A. (1987). Psychological Trauma. Washington DC: American Psychiatric Press, Inc.

Walz, B. (1990). General review of educational theory (lecture). Teaching Stress Concepts to Emergency Services Professions Conference August 6-9, 1990, Baltimore, Maryland

Warren, V.B. (Ed). (1964). A Treasury of Techniques for Teaching Adults. Washington, DC: National Association for Public Continuing and Adult Education.

Weimer, M. Parrett, J.L. and Kerns, M.M. (1988). How Am I Teaching? Forms and activities for acquiring instructional input. Madison, WI: Magna Publications.

Weimer, M. (Ed.). (1991). The guest Lecturer: Do's and Don't. Teaching Professor, 5(6): 2.

Yalom, I. (1985). Theory and practice of group psychotherapy (3rd ed.) New York: Basic Books.

I N D E X

Burnout 115

C

Caffeine 112
Case review 60, 178
Causes of CIS 139
Causes of stress 95
Certificates 133
Challenges 25
Chaplain program 3, 106
Chaplains 165
Character disorders 123
Chi-square analysis 211
Child abuse 66
Children 8
CIS 4
CISD 4, 5, 6, 7, 8, 9, 10, 103, 105, 151, 171, 175
CISD instructor 24
CISM 103, 105
CISM instructor 24
CISM / CISD course development 43
CISM / CISD students 22
CISM education 25
CISM instructors 24
CISM team 3, 105, 144
Clear and imminent danger 67
Clergy 15
Cognitive 136
Cognitive domain 39
Cognitive symptoms 102, 111
Command officers course on CIS 34
Command officers stress survival course 108, 114
Command officer's stress survival guide 106
Commercial 4, 6
Common critical incidents 140
Community groups 4
Community outreach 3
Conclusion 202
Confidentiality 67, 68
Conflict resolution 31
Consults 152

Distress **91, 92, 93, 96**
Domains of learning **38**

E

Educational value **68**
Effects of CIS **139**
Effects of stress **96, 102**
Elements of learning **36**
Emergency personality **143**
Emergency Services Stress **136, 138**
Emergency worker's suicide **102**
Emotional **136**
Emotional symptoms **102, 111**
Empirical Research Design **201**
Enabling objectives **45, 46**
Environment **34**
Epistemology **203**
Eustress **91, 92, 93, 95**
Evaluation **45**
Evaluation - level four **48**
Excessive media interest **8**
Exercise **97**
Experimental Mortality **210**
Experimental procedures **211**
External validity **211**
Extreme psychological distress **66**

F

Fact phase **173, 180**
Family life **97**
Family life services **3**
Follow up services **4, 127, 148, 153, 188**
Four step method of instruction **47**
Freeze frames **192, 193**
Function **176**

G

General **103**
General **114**
General Adaptation Syndrome **91, 92, 93, 96**
General cautions in teaching human elements **68**